Making the Most of your Inspection:
Primary

David Clegg
and
Shirley Billington

 The Falmer Press

(A member of the Taylor & Francis Group)
London • Washington, D.C.

UK   The Falmer Press, 4 John Street, London WC1N 2ET
USA   The Falmer Press, Taylor & Francis Inc., 1900 Frost Road,
        Suite 101, Bristol, PA 19007

First published 1994

A catalogue record for this book is available from the British Library

Library of Congress Cataloging-in-Publication Data are available on request

ISBN 0 7507 0247 8 paper

Jacket design by Caroline Archer

Typeset in 12/14 pt Bembo
by Graphicraft Typesetters Ltd., Hong Kong.

Printed in Great Britain by Burgess Science Press, Basingstoke on paper which has a specified pH value on final paper manufacture of not less than 7.5 and is therefore 'acid free'.

Contents

Acknowledgments

We would like to thank the Heads and teachers of Dorset primary schools especially those who have endured our presence on inspections. We are particularly grateful to those teachers who have contributed case study material.

Thanks also to those colleagues who have provided advice, support and constructive criticism. Any mistakes are entirely our own.

We owe an enormous debt of gratitude for the unflagging help and assistance provided by our support staff, in particular June Pinder and Chris Oram.

We are grateful to OFSTED for permission to use extracts from Inspection Reports.

Introduction

This book is about the new inspection arrangements for primary schools which come into force in September 1994. The book has two main aims — firstly, to put the new arrangements into some kind of perspective by explaining the details of the inspection procedures, and secondly, to help schools to gain the maximum professional benefit from the experience of inspection. The book is therefore a practical one which offers schools clear advice about planning and preparing for an inspection, so that they are able to incorporate the inspection into their own development plans and ensure positive outcomes. The book is not intended as a guide to bluffing your way through an inspection. Whilst it is written from the point of view of schools rather than inspectors, it does outline the context within which inspectors will work.

The focus for inspectors will be upon the educational outcomes achieved by the school, rather than the educational processes that the school employs. For example, inspectors will wish to be satisfied that pupils throughout the school can read to a satisfactory level, but will be less interested in the methods used by the school in teaching children to read. This is an important message for primary schools who may believe that inspectors are looking for a pre-conceived model of what is called 'good primary practice'. This is not the purpose of inspection.

The format of the book is such that individuals can refer to it for information and help without needing to read all the way through. The book covers all stages of inspection from notification through to responding to recommendations. The first chapter provides background information on the structure of an inspection and subsequent chapters deal with particular stages in the process. Each chapter begins with a brief introduction which outlines its contents. Some of the information contained within the book is not essential for schools in ensuring a successful inspection, but it is useful background reading.

As planning and preparing for an inspection is a major management task, the book reflects some management material that is already published and available and, where appropriate, it is referred to in the text. For this reason the book does not give detailed guidance on matters such as negotiating job descriptions, school development planning or producing schemes of work, but it does provide some notes and examples which some schools may find helpful. The advice offered in the book makes certain assumptions about the ways primary schools operate, particularly that to some extent responsibilities are shared, decisions are largely negotiated and that staff make every effort to work as a team. Having said that, the book emphasizes the crucial leadership role of the Headteacher. An important aspect of that role is working in partnership with the Governing Body which has a particular part to play in the inspection process. The book therefore suggests ways in which governors can be helped to manage their particular responsibilities.

The majority of the book takes the form of information or advice, but it also contains some case study material written by teachers and Headteachers who have had recent experience of inspections. This material appears within the text in the appropriate chapters and is used to illustrate and expand various points, providing an opportunity to dwell upon some individual experiences.

The book is aimed predominantly at Headteachers, but all teachers, especially senior managers would find it useful. It contains some information which governors should also find particularly helpful.

Chapter 1

The Structure of an Inspection

Introduction

This chapter focuses upon some of the background to the new OFSTED inspection arrangements. It will indicate the nature and purpose of an inspection and begin to explore in detail some of the procedures which will be common to all inspections.

The tendering process will be explained as will the various roles and responsibilities of members of the inspection team and senior members of staff.

The chapter will also make reference to the OFSTED Handbook for Inspection and will begin to demonstrate how the information within the Handbook can be used more effectively by schools.

In the last part of the chapter we look at what a school might gain from an inspection. The chapter is divided into the following sections:

- Nature and Purpose of the Inspection
- Tendering
- Roles and Responsibilities
- The Handbook for Inspection
- The Inspection Team
- The School Agenda

Nature and Purpose of the Inspection

A consistent feature of government policy to 'raise educational standards' has been the determination to separate those services designed to support, advise and develop schools from those designed to inspect them. It is this policy which has been one of the determinants of the government's approach to Local Education Authorities (LEAs) which traditionally have tried, with varying degrees of success, to fulfil both functions. It is not appropriate to reiterate the arguments for and against this approach here, but it is important that schools understand that the OFSTED approach to inspection reflects government policy. The purpose is not to support and advise, it is to collect a range of evidence, match the evidence against a statutory set of criteria, arrive at judgments and make those judgments known to the public. Put bluntly, OFSTED inspections are not designed to help individual schools to do a better job, they are designed to come to a judgment about the quality of the job which they are currently doing. Once the judgments are made and the report is written, it is the responsibility of the school, and in particular the governors, to come up with a plan to indicate how they will make any improvements deemed necessary by the inspection.

However, despite this approach, it is very likely that schools will be able to use the inspection as an opportunity to inform their own development. Staff and governors will receive a view of the school which will add to their own knowledge and will therefore contribute to a school's own self-evaluation. If self-evaluation is a significant feature of school development then perhaps school inspections will make a contribution to school improvement.

The nature of the inspection is largely set out in *The Handbook for the Inspection of Schools*, (the Handbook), which will guide the activities of the Reporting Inspector and the rest of the inspection team. All schools can obtain a copy of the Handbook from the Office for Standards in Education (OFSTED). The Handbook is a large document with several clearly marked sections, but only Part 2, 'The Framework for Inspection' contains statutory requirements. This is important as it means many elements of inspection, although subject to guidance and suggestions, are left to the discretion of individual Reporting Inspectors. These discretionary elements will lead to some variations in the precise way in which inspections are conducted.

However, one element over which inspectors and schools

will have very little control is the timing of the inspection. This will be dictated by several factors and will be subject to certain requirements, associated with the tendering process.

Tendering

It is the responsibility of Her Majesty's Chief Inspector (HMCI) to issue invitations for tenders. The invitations could be for an inspection of an individual school, or a cluster of phase specific schools. Schools due for inspection will be chosen completely at random, but in developing the current programme, HMCI have checked with LEAs to ascertain if any of the schools selected by OFSTED have had a recent LEA inspection. Inclusion on the list in the early stages does not necessarily indicate a school failing or at risk as was initially suggested. Given that during any academic year, 25 per cent of secondary schools and primary schools are to be inspected, random selection is the only possible method.

Before tenders are invited, HMCI will notify schools that they are to be included within the next inspection programme, and they will be asked to indicate any particular requests which fall outside the statutory framework, but which they would wish to be included in the inspection specification. For example, a school may have a nursery class or a particularly high proportion of children with special educational needs, both of which would require some specialist knowledge within the inspection team.

Figure 1 provides a broad outline of the pattern and timing of an inspection, assuming this will take place in the autumn term. Those schools to be inspected in the spring or summer will receive more notice since tenders will be issued for each academic year rather than each term. It is only Registered Inspectors, acting independently or on behalf of a company or LEA, who will be invited to tender for the inspection contracts. After expressing an interest, and before submitting a tender, Registered Inspectors will be sent the details of each of the schools to be included in the contract. These details will include any specific requirements which have been requested by individual schools. Registered Inspectors will also have to indicate the names of prospective

March	— Schools notified by HMCI that they will be included in the inspection programme for the following academic year. — Governors are asked if they have any particular requests regarding the inspection which fall outside the Framework for Inspection. These are entered on the Specification Form ('S' form).
April	— HMCI invite tenders for individual schools and/or clusters of phase specific schools within LEA boundaries. — Registered Inspectors submit tenders to HMCI including the names of the proposed team members.
June	— Contracts awarded to Registered Inspectors by HMCI.
July	— Reporting Inspector contacts school to negotiate inspection dates.
September	— Six weeks prior to inspection, Reporting Inspectors will contact schools, send out requests for information, including the 'Headteacher's form', and arrange a school visit three-four weeks prior to the inspection.
mid-October	— Inspection takes place.
November	— Report written, copies sent to school and HMCI. HMCI also receive record of evidence and the notes from the governors' meeting at which the inspection findings were presented.

Figure 1: Pattern and timing of an inspection

team members, including the Reporting Inspector and the Lay Inspector.

HMCI can only award a contract on the basis of competitive tendering. If, however, only one tender is submitted and this is judged by HMCI to be of good value, then the contract can be awarded. In the event of no tender being submitted after several invitations, the school will be inspected by HMI.

Contracts will be awarded on the basis of cost and quality. HMCI will scrutinize the tenders to ensure that the proposed team is suitably qualified in terms of phase and subject experience, and that team members are on the register of trained inspectors. Cost will also be a consideration, but this does not imply that the lowest figure will necessarily win the contract.

Roles and Responsibilities

Inspections will explore all aspects of school life, and will have some effect on virtually all those involved in school activities.

Within the school and the inspection team, there will be particular people with specific roles and responsibilities which may determine the success or otherwise of the inspection. If schools are to be well prepared for the inspection, then they need to be very clear about the roles played by key people.

Reporting Inspector (RI)[1] will be trained and registered as an inspector with OFSTED. S/he will have had a background in education, and in most cases will have experience of senior management in schools. S/he will have the major responsibility for coordinating the entire process. S/he will make contact with the school and collate and distribute the pre-inspection evidence to the appropriate members of the inspection team. S/he is likely to be the only member of the team to visit the school prior to the inspection and will be the major point of reference for the school during each stage. S/he will have the responsibility for coordinating the work of all inspectors, for feeding back to the school management and governors, for writing the final report and submitting it to HMCI. The Reporting Inspector will deal with any concerns or problems which the school has, before, during and after the inspection.

Team Inspectors will also be trained inspectors. Some team inspectors may be Registered Inspectors, but on this occasion be acting in the capacity of team members. They will also have a background in education, either as phase or subject specialists. They will be responsible for gathering evidence about particular curriculum areas and aspects of the school, and writing those parts of the report. They will also gather evidence about other whole school issues to submit to the Reporting Inspector. They may be responsible for giving feedback to the Head of Department or Curriculum Coordinator.

In each team, one member will be a **Lay Inspector** who will have no direct experience of school management. S/he will play a full part in the inspection process and will have a responsibility to report on a major area of school activity.

The Reporting Inspector will assume that the **Headteacher** has full responsibility for the school's internal management of the inspection. The relationship between the Head and the Reporting Inspector will be crucial in ensuring the smooth running of the inspection and it will be a major responsibility of the

Headteacher to keep staff briefed before the inspection, and to inform them of any changes during it. Headteachers will need to be sensitive to the anxiety and strain that inspection may cause amongst teaching staff and should see it as a major job to maintain morale, and ensure that staff keep the inspection in a proper perspective. Governors may also feel themselves under the spotlight and could need some reassurance. Whilst Headteachers will have the ultimate responsibility they should work closely with other senior managers. **Deputy Heads** should be assigned specific duties related to the inspection, and all **Heads of Department** and **Curriculum Coordinators** should be clearly briefed. We discuss the possible allocation of tasks in Chapter 3 'Preparing for Inspection'.

The **Chair of Governors** will have a key role in meeting with, and providing information for inspectors, as well as receiving and responding to the final report. S/he will need to have a good grasp of the inspection process, so that s/he is in a position to inform and support other governors.

The Handbook for Inspection

All inspections will follow a similar, but not identical, procedure. This procedure is largely defined in the Handbook, which is designed to cover all types of schools. The Handbook contains a variety of information, all of which could be useful to a school. However, the Handbook is written specifically for inspectors, rather than for schools, and is not especially helpful in providing advice and support to schools about managing the process. After the brief introduction, Part 2, The Framework, 'defines the standards inspectors have to meet'. It gives details about the range of evidence to be collected and the criteria against which judgments will be made. It also indicates the format of the report. It is important to understand that the Framework is the only part of the Handbook which is the subject of statutory procedures. It includes a code of conduct to which all inspectors must work (figure 2).

All the other sections of the Handbook (Parts 3–9) provide guidance. Some sections would be more helpful to schools than

The basic principles of the code are:

   (i)   honesty, clarity and consistency and impartiality in the framing and communication of judgments;

  (ii)   concern for accuracy and respect for evidence;

 (iii)   confidentiality in handling all information acquired during an inspection;

 (iv)   courtesy and fairness in dealing with all individuals and groups encountered in the course of an inspection;

  (v)   sensitivity to the circumstances of the school and of all individuals or groups connected with it;

 (vi)   respect for the integrity of teachers, pupils, parents and governors;

(vii)   recognition that the interests and welfare of pupils are the first priority in relation to anything inspectors observe or about which they are informed;

(viii)   sensitivity to the impact of judgments on others.

All inspectors are required to abide by this code of conduct when inspecting schools and to ensure that their inspection teams do so too.

Figure 2: Code of conduct for inspectors

others. The sections which illustrate specimen forms which the school will have to complete are useful, together with the Guidance: Inspection Organization and Inspection Schedules (Parts 3 and 4). The Inspection Schedules and Technical Papers (Part 5) amplify some of the criteria laid down in the Framework. The Handbook also gives further insights into how the inspection team will work, and provides information about some key aspects of the process. Some of this guidance will be amended, or changed in the light of experience. Part 2, of course, cannot be altered without a change to the law. The implications of this mixture of statutory framework and guidance, or put another way, legal procedures and discretionary elements, have already been mentioned, but it is worth stressing again. Reporting Inspectors will be guided by the Handbook, to a lesser or greater degree. This means that some of the processes of the inspection may be discussed and negotiated, and we will be examining some of those areas in Chapter 3.

The Inspection Team

The size of the inspection team will depend upon the size of the school. The Framework provides guidance on the minimum number of inspection days which different sized schools will be allocated. The smallest schools (less than fifty on roll), will have five days of inspection which would translate roughly into two inspectors for two-and-a-half days. The largest secondary schools (1500+ pupils) would have sixty days of inspector time. This figure could be divided between any number of inspectors, depending on the needs and requests of the school. The Reporting Inspector will give an indication as to how the days would be allocated and the proposed size of the team when submitting a tender. To some extent the number of inspectors will depend on the specialisms within the team. It may also be the case that not all inspectors will be in school for the full duration of the inspection. Some may spend three or four days out of a total of five, since their particular area would not require them to be there all the time.

This flexible approach is perhaps best seen by giving some possible examples:

Example 1 Large Primary School — 301–400 on roll
No. of days — 24

5 inspectors spend 4 days in school	20 days
2 inspectors spend 2 days in school	4 days

Total number of inspectors involved = 7
Total number of days = 24

Example 2 Small Primary School — 101–200 on roll
No. of days — 15

2 inspectors for 4 days	8 days
1 inspector for 3 days	3 days
2 inspectors for 2 days	4 days

Total number of inspectors involved = 5
Total number of days = 15

The majority of inspections will take place over one week, Monday to Friday.

As can be seen from the examples there are a number of possible combinations of team structures. The main criteria will be the ability of the team to cover all aspects of school activity as outlined in the Framework, as well as to respond to particular schools' requests. All inspection teams will have a balance between subject specialists and those who will have experience of whole school management, and these combinations will affect the team deployment.

In most cases, inspectors who have experience of whole school issues will also offer subject specialisms. Similarly, some inspectors will offer combinations of subject specialisms, such as history and geography, science and technology or expressive arts. At least one member of the team will have expertise in special educational needs. Where schools have pupils identified as having very specific special educational needs, perhaps taught within a unit, inspection teams will need to have someone with the appropriate experience. The combination of subject and whole school expertise will largely dictate the pattern of working.

Each member of the inspection team will be responsible for specific parts of the report, but the judgments made about whole school issues, such as the efficiency of the school and pupils' personal development and behaviour must represent the agreed judgments of the whole team. Every team member will be expected to collect evidence concerning the whole school, and cross-curricular issues.

The School Agenda

Finally in this chapter, it is important that we take a realistic look at what a school may hope to gain from the inspection. Much of what the school achieves will be the result of staff going through a shared experience, rather than the precise outcomes of the inspection. There are many Headteachers who have reflected upon inspection and are able to recognize it as a professionally rewarding experience for their schools. The reasons are varied but they include the following:

- a renewed sense of teamwork;
- an objective view of the school;

- confirmation that the school is largely successful;
- help in informing the next round of priorities;
- a boost for teaching staff;
- good publicity.

These reasons have something to do with the inspection itself, but much more to do with the way the school approached it, prepared for it, managed it, and responded to it. It is an important message that a school inspection is an activity which is able to engage the attention of the whole school and does provide an opportunity to get everyone thinking about and working towards a common goal.

The inspectors will be impressed (or not) by the way schools respond to the challenge of an inspection; they will notice how well staff and pupils are prepared, and will appreciate the co-operation and help they receive. There is no doubt that all inspection teams will be working to a very tight schedule, the agenda will be largely fixed, and inspections may be very different to those which LEAs have previously conducted. It will be up to individual schools to make the most of the opportunities provided by a full school inspection under the new arrangements.

Note

1   Throughout this book, the term Reporting Inspector refers specifically to the inspector leading the inspection. S/he must be a Registered Inspector, which is the term used in the Handbook, and is the equivalent of Reporting Inspector.

Chapter 2

The Inspection Process

Introduction

This chapter will explore the work of the inspection team, will give some indication of the format of the final inspection report and will also explain the use made of evidence collected prior to the inspection.

The chapter is divided into the following sections:

- The Responsibilities of the Inspection Team
- Pre-inspection Evidence
- The use of Quantitative Data
- Deployment of the Inspection Team
- Ways of Working
  — Classroom observations
  — Discussions with staff
  — Discussions with pupils
  — Examining pupils' work
- Putting Evidence Together
- Arriving at Judgments
  — Whole school issues
  — Subjects
- Completing the Record of Evidence
- Arriving at Main Findings

The Responsibilities of the Inspection Team

The inspection team will collect a wide range of evidence which will inform the final judgments made on a school. Such evidence includes statistical information, school documentation, classroom observations, discussions with parents, governors, staff and children and examining a range of pupils' work. The collection of evidence extends outside the actual period of inspection, and it is important to recognize that the preparatory stages of inspection provide a great deal of information which sets part of the agenda for the work of the team during the inspection week.

It is also important to recognize that judgments are firmly based on evidence, and that whilst some areas are the particular concern of individual inspectors, others will be a collective responsibility. Throughout the inspection period, there will be a great deal of discussion and exchange of information amongst the team in order to arrive at the main findings, for the school as a whole, and within particular curriculum areas.

Reporting Inspectors have a statutory responsibility to report on four main areas:

- the quality of education provided by a school;
- the standards achieved;
- the efficient use of resources;
- the spiritual, moral and cultural development of the pupils.

The final report will focus on these four areas, but will not be written to these headings. It must follow a set format, and will contain seven parts.

Parts 1 and 2 will include basic statistical information about the school together with the main findings of the inspection and the key issues for action.

Parts 3, 4 and 5 will focus on whole school issues and indicate overall judgments on standards of achievement and quality of learning, efficiency of the school and pupils' personal development and behaviour.

Part 6 will summarize judgments on provision in individual subjects.

Part 7 will provide judgments on all aspects of the school which impact upon Parts 3 to 6. These are:

- quality of teaching;
- assessment, recording and reporting;

- the curriculum
  — quality and range;
  — equality of opportunity;
- provision for pupils with special educational needs;
- management and administration;
- resources and their management
  — teaching and support staff;
  — resources for learning;
  — accommodation;
- pupils' welfare and guidance;
- links with parents, agencies and other institutions.

The summary of the report will contain basic information on the school, the main findings and key issues for action.

The methods used to examine these areas are described in some detail later in this chapter.

The Reporting Inspector has overall responsibility for arriving at judgments on a school, and must ensure that they are:

comprehensive, covering all aspects of the school, as defined in the Framework;

corporate, reflecting the collective view of the inspection team;

valid, based on direct observation and reflecting standards actually achieved;

secure, in that they are informed by quantitative data where possible.

Pre-inspection Evidence

Prior to an inspection, Headteachers will be required to complete a Headteacher's Form[1] for the information of the Reporting Inspector. This form will provide a range of statistical information on the school, relating to its organization, statutory assessment and examination results, accommodation, staffing and budget. Information will also be sought which will assist the team in placing the school in a national and local context. This includes detail of the area served, the ability range of the pupils, numbers of pupils with special needs or with English as a second language, and links with parents.

In addition to the Headteacher's form, schools will also need to complete the 'standards' questionnaire, which relates directly to the efficiency of the school. All schools will have received a copy of the questionnaire which is an appendix to the booklet *'Keeping your Balance'* (OFSTED, 1993). The document is also part of the Handbook.

The questionnaire serves three purposes:

(i)   it provides further pre-inspection information for Reporting Inspectors;

(ii) it gives clear criteria against which the efficiency of a school is to be judged;

(iii) it is a useful *aide-mémoire* for schools to review and evaluate their own efficiency.

Inspectors will base their view of a school's financial administration on the questionnaire, and the information will be checked during the course of the inspection.

The Headteacher's form and the 'standards' questionnaire, together with information provided to the Reporting Inspector on her/his visit, and the preliminary documentation supplied by the school, will, to some extent, influence the deployment of the inspection team and the schedule to which members will work.

> I received the written request for information and the inspection handbook before the holiday and had until 20 January to get it ready — that was when the Reporting Inspector was due to make a day visit to gather information and make the final arrangements for the inspection. The information required was very comprehensive even down to the number of fiction and non fiction books in school. The way that it was put to me was that the more information I could provide the easier it would be for the inspection team to prepare for the inspection and this would be reflected in the final report — a compelling argument.

I began to put together the information during the holiday — and carried on after the holiday. It took a long time but at least it made me complete a lot of things that had been sitting in my in-tray for a long time and because the information required was so comprehensive it made me think very hard about the school. I am sure that this helped me during the inspection week when I was questioned about all aspects of school life.

Headteacher

Prior to inspection, team members will analyze the information supplied by the school, and identify issues for inspection. The Record of Inspection Evidence collated by the Reporting Inspector will detail pre-inspection evidence and possible issues arising from it in sections which correspond to the format of the final report. A summary of the preliminary information gathered will be circulated to team members in advance of the inspection. This is to enable inspectors to have a clear focus for their work during the inspection period.

To give examples of the format of the Record of Evidence, figures 3 and 4 illustrate the pre-inspection comments, and issues for inspection which have been identified in two whole school issues.

The Use of Quantitative Data

Statistical information on a school, and comparison with similar types of schools locally and nationally, will provide the inspection team with some information on its context and performance. Inspectors will be provided with a range of performance indicators which will enable them to make some comparisons of a school's performance. The areas which will be set in a national context include:

- socio-economic data, such as the number of children on free meals;
- pupil-teacher ratio, and child-adult ratio;

7.3   THE CURRICULUM

7.3(i)   QUALITY AND RANGE OF THE CURRICULUM   Key Stage   : *1/2*

1   Pre-inspection commentary

: PTR is average. Some classes are vertically grouped to keep size of classes fairly even. No policy for class organization.

The only subject policy documents issued are for reading and writing.

Short and medium term planning is variable in form. There is a new school policy for topic planning. Short-term planning is quite detailed. Initiatives are being taken to improve continuity.

Continuity between Key Stages seems patchy — good in core subjects, non-existent in foundation.

Monitoring progress looks still to be a problem.

Overlap classes do not appear to plan collaboratively.

Timetables give little indication of what is being taught.

2   Issues for inspection

: Are the 'new' curriculum planning strategies helping teachers to improve the quality of work and of progression through the school?

Are teachers clearly identifying learning objectives and devising ways of meeting them effectively?

Is the 'record of work covered' a worthwhile activity for teachers to undertake at the end of each week? Would some form of evaluation be better?

Is the curriculum broad and balanced in most respects?

Check governors' responsibilities re curriculum — sex education, SEN, complaints procedure.

3   Main inspection evidence

:

Figure 3:   Record of evidence

- pupils' range of attainments on entry (where applicable);
- end of Key Stage assessment or examination results;
- teaching time available;
- average class/group size;
- attendance figures;
- budget allocation and unit costs per pupil;
- expenditure per pupil on books and equipment.

This information and the reference norms will appear at the beginning of the report.

7.6 (ii) RESOURCES FOR LEARNING

1   **Pre-inspection commentary**

: Money has been spent on repairs, maintenance and refurbishment. Parents' meeting expressed concern that it should be spent on resources for learning.

Resources areas and rooms have been organized by the Head to increase their effectiveness.

2   **Issues for inspection**

: Inspectors should examine the strengths and weaknesses of resource provision in relation to their subject assignments.

Is library provision adequate?

Are there any deficiencies?

Are libraries well used by pupils?

Are classes adequately stocked with basic equipment and books to support day to day work?

3   **Main inspection evidence**

:

Figure 4:   Record of evidence

National data for some of the areas listed is currently non-existent or very limited. The intention is that the national inspection programme will generate additional information which will enable some comparisons between schools of similar type. In other words a school should only be compared to schools of a similar nature. A school serving a socially disadvantaged urban community should not be compared in terms of standards of achievement to a school in an affluent leafy suburb. It should be compared to schools serving areas of similar disadvantage throughout the county.

Facts and figures and comparisons with other schools will not be the sole basis for judgments. Inspectors will look for a wide range of evidence which goes beyond raw statistics.

Deployment of the Inspection Team

The Reporting Inspector will plan the responsibilities of team members to ensure that all areas in the Schedule as outlined in

Section 2 of the Framework are covered. As previously discussed there will be some variation in team deployment, depending on the size and type of school. However, whatever the structure of the team, all will have some common ways of working.

During the inspection period, because time is limited, schools are asked to supply timetables in advance so that inspectors' programmes can be carefully planned. In many primary schools, the structure of the curriculum may result in parts of the school day being designated for 'integrated activities', 'topic work' or similar generic terms. The Reporting Inspector will ask for further detail of the planned activities, and it is helpful if class teachers can identify the main subject areas or focus of particular sessions.

For the purposes of inspection, it is helpful to all concerned to try to identify when particular subjects are being taught. Inspectors will understand that elements of the curriculum may be delivered through topics or themes, but within those sessions it is important to identify the main focus on specific subjects.

In some respects preparing for the inspection was harder for the teachers than for me because they were going to be the ones who had to 'perform' during the week. One issue we had to resolve was the timetable for the week — should we carry on as normal which would mean that we would not be able to show the inspectors all subjects in all classes or should we devise a timetable for the week that would include them all? In the end we compromised. I wanted to carry on as normal but I didn't want us to shoot ourselves in the foot and therefore we tried to fit in as much as we could without disrupting the pattern of the school. If I was involved in another inspection I think that I would go further in trying to include all subject areas because the inspectors were looking for evidence of the breadth of the National Curriculum throughout the school, but I would make it clear to the inspectors that the inspection week was atypical (the Reporting Inspector suggested that as far as possible we carry on as normal).

Headteacher

During the inspection period the main focus of all team members will be work in classrooms. Inspectors are expected to spend 75 per cent of the inspection period on classroom observations, and between them to see a representative sample of the work of the school. In order to achieve this, team members will be assigned to ensure that:

- approximately 20 per cent of lessons taught during the inspection period are observed (the figure will be less for a very large secondary school, greater for a small primary);
- the sample includes National Curriculum subjects for each age group of pupils of statutory school age;
- where there is ability grouping, a cross-section of groups is observed;
- subjects or courses outside the National Curriculum are included.

In addition to classroom observation, inspectors will have time planned for:

- discussions with staff, particularly those with management or curriculum responsibilities;
- discussions with pupils on an individual basis;
- examining a sample range of pupils' work.

The Reporting Inspector will consult with the Headteacher in advance of the inspection to agree times for talking with staff and examining pupils' work.

Ways of Working

Classroom Observations

Observation of classroom activities form a major part of the evidence on which cumulative judgments on a number of areas will be based. For each lesson, or part of a lesson seen, an observation pro-forma will be completed by the visiting inspector.

Summary Details
- to include subject/activity, size of class, age and ability range, length of time observed.

Content of Lesson
- a brief description of the content and organization of the activities observed.

Standards of Achievement — in relation to national norms
- comparison of pupils' achievement with national levels   Grade ☐

Standards of Achievement — in relation to pupils' capabilities
- opportunities for pupils to display their skills, knowledge and understanding;
- pupils' competence across the curriculum in literacy, oracy and numeracy.   Grade ☐

Quality of Teaching
- an assessment of the effectiveness of the teaching methods used and the teacher's competence in handling the lesson;
- the planning and presentation of activities;
- the setting of appropriate goals for groups and individuals;
- the suitability of content and the involvement of pupils.   Grade ☐

Quality of Learning
- identifiable gains in pupils' knowledge, skills and understanding;
- pupils' competence as learners;
- development of learning skills.   Grade ☐

Contribution to Achievements in other areas
- references or opportunities to develop knowledge or skills in other subjects or cross-curricular themes;
- application of cross-curricular skills.

Contributory Factors
- the positive or negative influences on the work seen of:
  — accommodation
  — resources
  — support staff   Overall Lesson Grade ☐

Figure 5: Lesson observation notes

Observation schedules are in standard form and include descriptive elements, judgments and numerical grades on the quality of teaching, learning and pupils' standards of achievement. Each lesson is given an overall grade based on the grades of these three areas. Observation schedules are divided into seven sections, and the main areas for comment and evaluation are indicated below (figure 5).

Inspectors are required to use a five point grading scale to judge the main elements of each lesson observed. The grade descriptions are outlined in the Handbook and range from 1 (very good) to 5 (poor) for standards of achievement, quality of learning and quality of teaching. On rare occasions, mixed evidence may make final grading misleading, in which case grade 6 (conflicting evidence) will be used.

Pupils' standards of achievement must also be graded in relation to national standards, again on a five point scale. These range from 1 (high) to 5 (low). The emphasis on judging standards highlights the requirement for inspections to focus on educational outcomes, in this instance in terms of pupil achievement.

Good practice (grade 2) is expected to be attainable in most, if not all, schools, but unsatisfactory practice (grade 4) may also be found in many schools. The intention of grading is not to focus on individual lessons, but to contribute to a systematic analysis of the overall findings about key features of a school in terms of the quality of teaching and learning, as well as provision in particular subjects.

Discussions with Staff

Headteachers, Deputy Heads and most teachers carrying a management or curriculum responsibility can expect to be interviewed by a member of the inspection team. Headteachers and Deputies, by virtue of their multiple responsibilities, may be seen by more than one inspector. Other members of staff, teaching and non-teaching, may be required to discuss their particular roles and contribution to the school. Job descriptions will form a useful basis for the areas to be discussed, which will obviously vary according to the nature of an individual's post. In general terms, for example, teachers with curriculum responsibilities can expect inspectors to seek information as follows:

Have you attended any recent INSET?

What opportunities do you have to carry out your responsibilities?

Have you had any support from external agencies or advisory staff?

Have you had any opportunities for leading curriculum development throughout the school?

Have you got any budget responsibilities?
How do you contribute to teachers' planning?

Some of the discussion will focus on the provision of whole school policy or guidelines covering this particular area.

For non-teaching staff, inspectors will be interested in exploring the following questions, through discussions with individuals, as well as through observation of their work.

Do non-teaching staff have clear guidance?
Is their expertise fully utilized?
Are they effectively deployed?
Are they used to facilitate effective use of teacher time?

Discussions with Pupils

These are likely to take place during the course of classroom observations, although there may be some instances of pupils being withdrawn for specific activities, such as reading or to talk about samples of their work. In classrooms, inspectors will want to gather and check information which will contribute to their judgments on the quality of learning provided, and pupils' standards of achievement. Inspectors will be interested in the following:

- pupils' understanding of the task(s) set;
- how it relates to other work they have done;
- the extent of knowledge gained by pupils;
- opportunities for them to develop competence in skills across the curriculum;
- the appropriateness of the task(s) for individual pupils;
- their degree of interest and motivation;
- their ability to evaluate their work;
- their ability to concentrate, cooperate and work productively with others.

Examining Pupils' Work

At an early stage in the inspection, the team will want to see a representative sample of pupils' past, recent and current work.

This provides an opportunity to set current work in a longer-term context. Inspectors will want to see examples of work which:

- cover all curriculum areas;
- represent the age range across the school;
- reflect the range of ability levels.

Inspectors will be aware that many activities may be undertaken by pupils which do not result in recorded work. For this reason they will also be interested in portfolios, Records of Achievement, pupil profiles and teacher records.

In examining these sources of evidence, inspectors will be looking at:

- overall progress by pupils;
- the pace of learning;
- the range of tasks set in particular subjects;
- examples of diffcrentiated tasks;
- standards of presentation;
- marking strategies;
- progression and continuity within a particular curriculum area.

Putting Evidence Together

Throughout the inspection, team members as individuals and collectively, will begin to put together a range of information in order to formulate their judgments. Observations and collection of factual information will enable inspectors to answer some of the questions raised as issues for inspection in the Record of Evidence.

Some aspects of the school can be examined very early in the inspection, and judgments will quickly be reached on, for example:

- accommodation — state of repair, use, particular features or deficiencies;
- attendance — pupil punctuality, registration procedures;

- resources — range, suitability, accessibility;
- organization — school routines, communication systems;
- pupil behaviour — relationships, discipline, opportunities to take responsibility.

In all teams some whole school aspects will be the responsibility of individual inspectors, whilst others will be the collected views of the team. There will be some variation in the way this is organized, but it is probable that in most teams, the following areas will be given to individuals:

- assessment, recording and reporting (see Appendix 1);
- special educational needs (see Appendix 2);
- resources — accommodation
          — teaching and support staff
          — resources for learning;
- equal opportunities;
- school efficiency.

Whilst individuals may be responsible for collating information on a particular area, all areas will be the subject of team discussion with the intention of arriving at agreed judgments.

The Reporting Inspector will specify those areas to which all team members are expected to contribute. Much of the information will be gathered in the course of classroom visits and observations around the school. These areas could include:

- pupils' spiritual, moral, social and cultural development;
- behaviour and discipline;
- quality of learning;
- quality of teaching;
- quality and range of the curriculum.

Arriving at Judgments

The Handbook contains a section on Guidance; Inspection Schedule (Part 3), which outlines the criteria against which judgments should be made. The section follows the format of the report and amplifies the evaluation criteria contained in the Framework. Each part of the Guidance commences with two contrasting summary statements, identifying firstly good, and secondly unsatisfactory, features relating to a particular area.

Inspectors will use these as a guide in making judgments, and will look for some indicators in each area, rather than expecting all features of good or unsatisfactory practice to be present.

Each section in the Guidance also outlines the issues for consideration when reviewing evidence, and features to be taken into account when reaching a judgment. A look through the Guidance will show that evidence for some areas can be collected fairly readily. Other areas will require more time, and perhaps considerable discussion amongst the team before judgments can be made.

There are some differences in the methods used for collecting evidence on whole school issues, and on subjects. The former tend to focus very much on established policies and procedures, and there will be a considerable bank of information for particular areas which will be acquired before or during the early stages of inspections. The exceptions here are quality of learning and quality of teaching, and overall standards of achievement, to which classroom observations, staff discussions and examination of pupils' work make a major contribution.

In collecting evidence on individual subjects, key elements are classroom based activities and lesson observation notes. Other related activities include discussions with coordinators, looking at documentation and examining teachers' planning.

To illustrate the various ways of collecting evidence and arriving at judgments, we look at the information required and methods of acquiring it, for two whole school issues, and then for a subject.

Whole School Issues

The following charts (figures 6 and 7) give an outline of two areas to be inspected. Each identifies some possible features of the area upon which inspection might focus, and gives some examples of evidence of each feature and ways in which it might be collected.

Feature inspected	Possible sources of evidence	May be provided by
• administrative procedures	• staff handbook • information for parents • timetables	• school documentation
• communication systems	• pattern of meetings • staff notice board • use of 'day book'	• pre-inspection information • observations in school
• school systems and routines	• guidance for staff • notices in classrooms • letters home	• observations in school • discussions with staff and pupils
• planning systems	• School Development Plan • action plans • budget allocation	• school documentation • discussions • minutes of meetings
• quality of leadership	• job descriptions • aims and objectives • shared values and understandings	• documentation • discussions at all levels — governors, staff, parents, pupils

Figure 6: Management and administration (Section 7.5 of report)

The examples are illustrative rather than definitive. Schools differ greatly, and therefore sources of evidence will vary, as will methods of collecting it. In arriving at a judgment on the effectiveness of the management and administration of a school the team will be looking for:

- a positive ethos;
- a clear sense of direction;
- clearly established day-to-day routines and procedures;
- clearly understood roles and responsibilities;
- an understanding on the part of all those (staff, children, parents) affected by systems and routines;
- general orderliness in the way the school runs;
- systems for communication.

Documentation provided prior to the inspection, information on school procedures, observation of routines and movement around the school, together with discussions, should enable a team to arrive at an early judgment on this area of school life. In arriving at judgments on curriculum provision, inspectors will be looking for:

Feature inspected	Possible sources of evidence	May be provided by
• planning for teaching and learning	• year group or class-based topic plans • teachers' weekly/daily plans	• planning documents (seen pre-inspection or on visits to classrooms) • discussions with teachers and pupils
• planning for continuity and progression	• long and short term planning (subject or class) • children's work • records of pupil experiences	• documentation • classroom visits • review of work across school
• planning for breadth and balance	• time allocated to individual subjects • provision for cross-curricular themes and dimensions	• timetables • curriculum audit • observation of teaching • discussions
• planning for individual subjects	• Schemes of Work • links with National Curriculum	• curriculum documentation • School Development Plan
• organization of pupils	• class organization • arrangements for grouping of pupils • provision of additional support	• Headteacher's Form • classroom observation • SEN support

Figure 7: Quality and range of curriculum (Section 7.3(i) of report)

- some evidence of breadth, balance, differentiation and relevance;
- planning to meet National Curriculum requirements;
- a match between planning and practice;
- recognition of curriculum entitlement and arrangements for equality of access for all pupils;
- planning for continuity and progression in pupils' experience;
- the effectiveness of curricular organization at classroom level, particularly in mixed age classes;
- some systems for curriculum review and evaluation;
- the level of involvement of the Governing Body.

Judgments on the quality and range of the curriculum cannot be made at an early stage of inspection. Lesson observations will make an important contribution to assessing the effectiveness of curriculum planning.

The Guidance makes a very clear statement about a school having responsibility to decide on the way the curriculum is organized. Inspection teams should have no preconceived notions about a curriculum framework. Their task is to judge the effectiveness of curriculum planning in advancing pupil learning, regardless of the model of organization.

Subjects

Each inspection report has to include judgments on standards of work in each National Curriculum area. As well as a comment on standards achieved throughout the school, the report must also include comments on each Key Stage, where applicable, and on the extent to which statutory requirements are being met.

Some sources of evidence, which provide a context for arriving at judgments on a particular subject, have already been discussed. These include any plans for review and development on the School Development Plan, relevant curriculum documentation, the role of the coordinator, and individual teachers' planning. Inspectors will also be interested in the provision and management of resources, and arrangements for assessment and record-keeping for each subject.

In arriving at judgments on standards achieved, the major source of evidence is lesson observation notes. The gradings given for all lessons observed for the quality of learning, the quality of teaching, standards achieved, and the overall grades, will be collated to provide data for final judgments.

As part of the Record of Evidence, inspectors have to complete subject evidence forms. These record judgments on the standards achieved in, and the management of, individual subjects. The sheets include a summary of the grades given to all lessons observed. The subject evidence forms are quite detailed, and require inspectors to summarize the strengths and weaknesses in the teaching of each subject, and in each Key Stage. The first part of the subject evidence forms will focus on standards and quality in learning and teaching. To give an example, a subject evidence form for English might include the data, and comments as detailed in figure 8. In addition to standards of achievement, quality of learning and quality of teaching, judgments have to be made on five factors which contribute to the management of a subject:

(i)   curriculum — organization, planning, match with National Curriculum, provision for all pupils;

(ii) assessment, recording and reporting — the effectiveness of the school's system, recording of attainment in National Curriculum;

(iii) staffing — use of staff expertise, support and guidance for teachers, the contribution of support staff, if applicable;

(iv) resources — organization, accessibility and use, budgeting, any health and safety issues;

(v)   accommodation — use of available space, any constraints through inappropriate accommodation, any plans for improvements.

Completing the Record of Evidence

Throughout the inspection period, the team will be meeting regularly to discuss their findings and to start to form judgments. Subjects will be the concern of individual inspectors, although other members of the team will contribute some information and observations.

Completion of the Record of Evidence for whole school issues is likely to be the responsibility of the Reporting Inspector. As indicated earlier, some whole school issues will be allocated to individual team members. The expectation is that they will take the lead in collecting relevant evidence and formulating judgments. However, each area will be the subject of discussion at a team meeting and all members will contribute information. The inspector responsible may modify judgments in the light of colleagues' observations. Inspection team meetings will have a set agenda as well as time for some general discussion. Those areas on which judgments may be made at an early

A separate form should be used to summarize each subject or aspect of the curriculum inspected.

SUBJECT or ASPECT INSPECTED: ENGLISH

Time spent observing lessons during inspection

Key Stage	Pre-1	1	2	3	4	VI form
Total (hours)	1h 10m	4h 30m	4h 40m			

3.1 STANDARDS OF ACHIEVEMENT

Achieve Grade	1	2	3	4	5	6
No. of lessons		5	9	3	1	

Standards overall range from good to unsatisfactory across the school. Standards in reading are generally good in both Key Stages, though in Key Stage 2 pupils need more opportunity to develop information retrieval skills. Standards in writing and spelling are satisfactory in Key Stage 1, but unsatisfactory in all aspects of written work at Key Stage 2.

Standards of presentation in written work in all subjects are variable. Much of the work in pupils' books is unsatisfactory but where written work is displayed around the school, presentation is generally better, and word processing is used to good effect.

Standards in speaking and listening are generally satisfactory, and good in a few classes in both Key Stages. Pupils are generally confident in speaking, and most are attentive listeners.

3.2 QUALITY OF LEARNING

Teach Grade	1	2	3	4	5	6
No.		7	7	5	1	

The quality of learning is satisfactory, and in some instances good, in Key Stage 1. It is generally unsatisfactory in Key Stage 2, except for those pupils receiving support in a small group setting, where learning is good.

The quality of learning in reading is good. Pupils have frequent opportunities to read, or to have books read to them, and most parents are involved in hearing their children read at home. Pupils demonstrate a high level of interest and enjoyment in books, and are generally confident readers. Older pupils in Key Stage 2 need more opportunity to become critical readers and to develop skills in using reference books.

In written work, where the activity has purpose and pupils are encouraged to extend their thinking and to apply their skills in spelling and handwriting, learning is good. It is usually unsatisfactory where written work involves the completion of isolated exercises, or copying texts.

Pupils have regular handwriting lessons, but there needs to be an increased emphasis on developing correct letter formation, good pencil grip and an appropriate position when writing. Few pupils transfer skills practised in handwriting sessions to other aspects of their written work.

6.1 QUALITY OF TEACHING

Teach Grade	1	2	3	4	5	6
No.		9	5	5	1	

The quality of teaching is generally good at Key Stage One, and unsatisfactory at Key Stage 2.

> Teaching is good where there is a clear explanation of the task, pupils are given examples of what is expected of them, work is well-matched to pupils' needs and teachers' expectations are high. It is frequently unsatisfactory where the whole class is set the same task, often involving copying from the blackboard or completing worksheets which are inappropriate for many pupils.
>
> Where bilingual pupils, or those with special educational needs are supported in small groups, teaching is good.

Figure 8: Subject evidence form

stage, will be the subject of discussion at a team meeting on possibly the second day of inspection. If evidence is clear at this stage and judgments are agreed, the Reporting Inspector may then complete the Record of Evidence.

So to follow through examples given earlier in the chapter (figure 8), the Record of Evidence for Resources for Learning might be completed as follows (figure 9), when further evidence has been gathered in school. For those areas identified as being a team responsibility, discussion is likely to be led by the Reporting Inspector. Some whole school issues will be discussed at early team meetings and at a later stage, will be an agenda item. The Reporting Inspector will complete the Record of Evidence and write the relevant section for the report.

All principal judgments made by the team will be summarized on two judgment recording forms. One is concerned with whole school issues, the second with specific subjects. Examples of the forms can be found as Appendices 1 and 2 of Part 7 of the Handbook.

Although recording judgments on a sliding scale may appear rather simplistic, it is important to be aware that the form has two main purposes. Firstly to focus the discussion of the inspection team on the judgments which it needs to make. Secondly, to ease the processing of information by OFSTED, and provide some summary information on national trends.

Arriving at Main Findings

The main findings of any inspection emerge gradually in a variety of ways. The frequent team meetings enable inspectors to compare findings and judgments, to share views, and to agree to

---

7.6(ii) RESOURCES FOR LEARNING

1   Pre-inspection commentary

: Money has been spent on repairs, maintenance and refurbishment. Parents meeting expressed concern that it should be spent on resources for learning.

Resources areas and rooms have been organized by the Head to increase their effectiveness.

2   Issues for inspection

: Inspectors should examine the strengths and weaknesses of resource provision in relation to their subject assignments.

Is library provision adequate?

Are there any deficiencies?

Are libraries well used by pupils?

Are classes adequately stocked with basic equipment and books to support day to day work?

3   Main inspection evidence

Resources are well maintained and accessible.

Classrooms are generally appropriately resourced for age/ability ranges.

Most curriculum areas are well-resourced.

Newly-established libraries are well-organized. Good range of fiction books, very few information books for Key Stage 1, well-resourced in Key Stage 2.

Libraries are under-used.

Equipment for role play in the nursery unit and in reception classes is very shabby.

Figure 9

clarify issues or to seek further evidence during the inspection. These processes are important in ensuring that the main findings represent a collective view of a school's strengths and weaknesses.

The evidence base which is generated during inspection is critical in formulating the overall judgments on a school. Where evidence is limited, this will be indicated within the report, or where a subject is not being taught at the time of the inspection, this will be clearly stated.

In arriving at overall judgments on standards and quality achieved, the data produced in the course of class observations will be the key feature. The Reporting Inspector will need to take into account the findings on each subject area, and each Key Stage, to reach a cumulative verdict on overall standards.

The inspection team is required to give greatest weight in the main findings to standards, efficiency and the overall quality of the school. Whilst the Reporting Inspector needs to be aware of the strength of the evidence available for judgements made, s/he is clearly required to focus on the outcomes rather than the contributory factors which may influence these.

Having said that, the report should attempt to set the school in some kind of context. Apart from the national and local comparative data, within the main findings there will be references to individual school circumstances which should affect a school's achievements. So, for example, high staff turnover, exceptional socio-economic disadvantage or severe budget constraints may be mentioned in this section.

Note

1   A specimen copy of a Headteacher's Form can be found in the Handbook.

Reference

OFSTED (1993). *Keeping your Balance — Standards for Financial Administration in Schools*, London, OFSTED and the Audit Commission.

Chapter 3

Preparing for Inspection

Introduction

The preparatory stage is very important and needs to be carefully planned and managed if schools are to make the most of the inspection itself. At this stage of the process it is important that the Headteacher emphasizes to all those involved that the school has an active part to play in the inspection. Indeed, there will be an expectation on the part of the inspectors that the school may have some specific issues that the inspection could take into account.

This chapter offers advice on planning and organizing the pre-inspection period. We suggest the appropriate action to take on receiving initial notification of inspection, the steps to be taken to inform the various groups who will be involved, and the development of an appropriate strategy for managing the process. The chapter is divided into the following sections in order to give a clear guide to managing the preparatory stages:

- Notification
- Informing People Involved:
  — Teaching staff
  — Governors
  — Non-teaching staff
- Managing the Preparation:
  — Allocating roles and responsibilities
  — Role of head and deputy
  — Review of routine procedures
  — Timetable of events
  — Action plan

- Documentation
  — Basic data
  — General information
  — Staffing
  — Curriculum
  — Assessment
- The Involvement of Parents
  — Informing Parents
  — Explaining their role
  — Documenting parental involvement
  — Briefing
- The Parents' Meeting
- Action Check List

The chapter ends with a sample check list which Headteachers may find useful in planning the school's preparation.

Notification

Just before Christmas I had a phone call informing me that we were to be inspected during the week beginning 8 February — just what I needed at the end of term, couldn't they have waited until after Christmas and let me have the holiday in blissful ignorance of what was to come? I have never been part of an HMI inspection before but from what I had been told they had assumed an almost mythical quality with tales of how difficult they were for all concerned. Should I tell the staff and spoil their holiday too? I asked several of the teachers who I thought could cope with the news, they advised me to tell everyone, the reason being that teams might wish to meet during the holiday to plan next term's work.

In retrospect I am glad that I did, I prefer to work in an open way and to have hidden it until after the holiday would have given the wrong message. I know that we are not perfect but I believe that this is a good school with a good staff and I don't believe that we have anything to hide, on the contrary I think we have things to show.

Part of me was even looking forward to the inspection

— it was put to me as 'the best INSET you will ever get' and the idea of a team of high powered inspectors in school for a week was quite exciting — we don't see many inspectors these days and I thought that being able to discuss some of the issues that we have been wrestling with would be beneficial to us all.

Headteacher

When the letter arrives informing you that your school is to be inspected, do not panic! Your attitude as the Headteacher, your response to this information, and the manner in which you share it with staff, governors and parents, will set the tone for the whole inspection process.

There is some useful information in the Handbook which will be helpful in enabling you to plan in the long and short term for the inspection.

Time should be taken to plan a strategy for managing the preliminary stages. It will be important to involve senior staff in sharing the responsibility for planning and preparation. Senior staff will be for some primary schools, the Deputy Head, or equivalent. In larger schools, it will mean the senior management team. An early discussion with this group will enable Headteachers to share information, to decide how all other staff will be informed, and to begin to develop a timescale for action during the pre-inspection period.

Sharing the information available in the Handbook will help senior staff to develop an overview of the inspection process, and to plan with the Headteacher for the briefing of their colleagues.

Briefing the teaching staff at an early stage is important in enabling them to overcome initial apprehension, to begin to reach an understanding of what will be involved, and the part which they will play in the process.

It will also be important at this stage to inform the Local Education Authority (where appropriate), and your Chair of Governors. He or she will also need some guidance on what inspection involves, and the part which governors will need to play in the proceedings. It may be helpful to invite him or her to the briefing meeting for staff.

Informing People Involved

Teaching Staff

Teaching staff should be informed as soon as possible, following detailed discussions with senior staff. All teachers will be involved in the inspection, and for most, it will be a new and rather daunting experience. It is important therefore that the circumstances in which they are told are given some careful thought. We have stressed that speed is important. This is not the kind of information that Headteachers would want to be the subject of rumour and speculation.

Notification of the inspection may conveniently coincide with a planned staff meeting, but if this is not the case then a specific meeting should be called. Headteachers will use their judgment, but it may be useful to invite the Chair of Governors to this meeting.

Headteachers need to be clear about the purposes of this first meeting, which should certainly include the following:

(i) to introduce the inspection in a positive way and allay any anxieties;
(ii) to give a clear account of the inspection process;
(iii) to begin to explain what impact the inspection will make on individual teachers.

Introducing the inspection
Some brief background information regarding the new national arrangements will explain how inspections will become an increasingly common experience for schools. It may be helpful to emphasize that being chosen for inspection has no special significance, as schools are selected at random.

The inspection should be presented as an opportunity to gain a new perspective on the school from a group of professionals who will have a wide range of relevant experience. Those schools which already have a well-defined and efficient system of self-evaluation or internal review will see the inspection as making a major contribution to their own activities.

What were my professional expectations?

Certainly not to use the Inspection Report as a stick with which to beat the staff. However, there was almost a masochistic pleasure in having an objective and professional in-depth look at the school. We knew it would be a rigorous week and I was concerned that the staff should endeavour to behave in as normal a manner as possible. I also hoped there would be things in the report about which we could 'celebrate'. I firmly believe that this is a good school and I hoped that in these times of 'media-hype' about standards etc., there would be positive things which could be written about. I wanted a series of comments which would reflect where further development was necessary. This was vital to the SDP and to the school as a whole. I even highlighted areas of concern to the Reporting Inspector prior to the inspection in the hope of further investigation within the week — Assessment and Mathematics were two such areas. This was no secret, as I had already discussed this with the staff on many occasions. Happily, the Reporting Inspector was able to oblige.

Headteacher

The inspection process

Teachers will need a clear outline of what an inspection entails, and the various procedures before, during and after the inspection team's visit. The various phases of inspection, the inspectors' code of conduct and the timescale to which the school and inspection team need to work, should be shared with teachers to enable them to gain a view of all that inspection involves. It may be helpful for teachers to have the various stages of inspection presented in the form of a flow chart (figure 10). Teachers should also have some background information regarding the inspection team.

Details of the composition of the team will become clearer at the meeting with the Reporting Inspector.

Notification of inspection	Consultation with governors. 'S' form sent and returned.
Reporting Inspector makes contact, negotiates inspection dates and requests data and information	The precise nature of this data and information is outlined in the Handbook.
Preliminary visit by Reporting Inspector	This will be an opportunity to become more familiar with the composition of the team, and any particular expertise the members may have. Reporting Inspector will collect information and talk with staff.
Pre-inspection parents' meeting arranged	All parents will be invited to comment about the school. A sample questionnaire which can be sent to parents is contained in the Handbook. The parents' meeting will be chaired by the Reporting Inspector, who will be concerned to gain parental views covering a range of school issues.
Inspection period	This will take the form of: • Classroom observations • Discussions and interviews with teachers, helpers, pupils and governors • Looking at documentation
Verbal feedback to Head and senior staff	Feedback may be given to senior teachers together or individually. Inspectors will begin to outline the main points of the report which will form the basis of feedback to the governors. Factual information to be contained within the report will be checked.
Verbal feedback to Governing Body and Head	This will be an opportunity for the governors to consider their response to the inspection and what may need to be included in their action plan.
Written report to school and HMCI	Evidence collected during the inspection will be sent with the report to HMCI. Schools should receive the written report within five weeks of the inspection.
Governing body to produce an action plan in response to the recommendations	It is probable that the governors will rely heavily upon the Head and staff to produce a detailed action plan responding to the key points in the report.

Figure 10: Stages of inspection

Impact on individual teachers

The inspection will affect all staff in various ways. As all teachers should have some curriculum responsibility, there will be two main areas of focus:

1 **The nature of their curriculum responsibility**

   Points for discussion have been outlined in the previous chapter.

   For those teachers who have a responsibility which covers the whole curriculum, such as coordinators for assessment, curriculum planning or special needs provision, inspectors will be interested in their impact across the school and their links with curriculum coordinators.

2 **Their work as class teachers**

   Inspectors will expect curriculum plans, lesson plans and pupil records including any relevant test scores to be available when they visit classrooms.

Being observed will inevitably be a little stressful, but it would be unwise to radically change a teaching style for the purpose of the inspectors' observation. Essentially the message for teachers is to teach in the way you normally do and be yourself.

Governors

Whatever the decision about inviting the Chair of Governors to attend the staff meeting, it is vital that she/he is informed immediately about the impending inspection. It would be advisable to do this face to face rather than by letter, since this will provide an opportunity to put the inspection into a proper context.

An early meeting of the Governing Body should be briefed in a similar way to the staff. Governors should understand that inspectors will gain some preliminary information about their activities through reading the minutes of recent governors' meetings and a copy of their last annual report to parents. Inspectors will want to have some discussions with governors on their response to recent legislation and their involvement in school activities. Judgments will be made on the Governing Body's effectiveness in fulfilling its statutory responsibilities. It is important

that governors are also aware that they have a specific responsibility to receive, and to respond to, the final report.

During this meeting, it would be worth trying to arrange
a date for a governors' meeting during the week following the
inspection for the Headteacher to report back on the main findings, and to prepare the Governing Body for the official feedback
from the Reporting Inspector.

Non-teaching Staff

The inspection will affect non-teaching staff in various ways. It
is certainly important that they are kept informed and briefed as
to what they may expect during the inspection period. Essentially,
the inspectors will judge whether all non-teaching staff are used
as effectively as possible, and are able to make appropriate con-
tributions to the work of the school.

Managing the Preparation

To make sure that the pre-inspection period goes as smoothly
as possible, a clear action plan should be devised. This will re-
inforce positive attitudes and will instil a feeling of confidence in
all staff. The action plan should be formulated after the initial
staff meeting, so that any particular concerns that emerge can be
incorporated into the detailed planning. This should be done in
consultation with the Deputy Head. This is particularly important not only in terms of the professional development of the
Deputy Head, but also as, in the event of the Headteacher being
absent for any reason, the inspection would still take place.

An important early task is to review, and possibly to revise,
any immediate school development plans. It would be unrealistic
to expect major initiatives and developments to continue un-
affected during the run-up to inspection.

The following areas should be the focus of an action plan:

(i)   allocating roles and responsibilities
(ii) roles of Head and Deputy
(iii) review of routine procedures
(iv) timetable of events

Allocating Roles and Responsibilities

Although the Head will play the major role in managing this process he or she should not become over-burdened. There is scope for delegation, particularly to the Deputy and also to other senior members of staff. However, the Headteacher will obviously have a key role in gathering together basic information and in liaising directly with the Reporting Inspector.

The 'Framework for the Inspection' provides a useful starting point for allocating roles and responsibilities. Using the Framework will ensure that areas from which evidence will be gathered during the inspection are looked at systematically. Teachers who are allocated specific responsibilities should be very clear about the nature of those responsibilities. They will include the following:

- gaining a detailed knowledge of the relevant section within the Framework;
- collating available documentation;
- providing support and advice for colleagues.

At this stage, Headteachers should make it clear to teachers with responsibilities that it would not be appropriate to undertake major curriculum or organizational changes.

The following is a possible allocation of responsibilities based on some of the headings in the Framework.

Headteacher:	efficiency of the school
	pupils' personal development and behaviour
	management and administration
	resource management (staff)
	links with parents, agencies and other institutions
Deputy Head:	equality of opportunity
	quality and range of curriculum
	resources for learning
	accommodation
Assessment Coordinator:	assessment, recording and reporting

> **SEN Coordinator:** provision for pupils with special needs
> **Curriculum** curriculum content, organization and
> **Coordinators:** planning

Clearly these responsibilities will be delegated in a way which reflects the school's staffing structure. For example, those schools which have a system of year leaders, rather than curriculum coordinators, will arrange things differently. The main point is, responsibilities should be clearly defined. However the responsibilities are allocated, it is important that each individual has a copy of the relevant section within the Framework, which will provide a clear picture of the criteria and evidence which will guide inspectors.

Roles of Head and Deputy

Briefing coordinators
Within the delegation of responsibilities, it is important to highlight some additional tasks which the Head and Deputy will need to undertake. A particular task will be to provide a detailed briefing for each teacher who has been allocated a responsibility from the list above. Some of this can be done collectively, but there may be a need for individual discussion and support, particularly for less experienced coordinators. Specific reference should be made to sections of the Framework which detail the evaluation criteria to be applied to each area. For those teachers with a curriculum responsibility, reference should be made to those parts of the Framework which specify the evaluation criteria to be applied to individual subjects. These are summarized below:

- standard of pupil achievement;
- quality of learning;
- quality of teaching;
- arrangements for assessing and recording progress in each subject;
- subject planning and organization;
- managing the subject;

- quality of resources;
- accommodation.

Sound knowledge of the criteria will enable all coordinators to begin a systematic review of the organization of their subject. This review will provide an opportunity to clarify any inconsistencies and to advise and support colleagues.

Meeting with Reporting Inspector
The initial meeting between the Head and Reporting Inspector is a particularly important occasion. It is an opportunity to establish a professional relationship, upon which the inspection process will build. The Reporting Inspector will have a particular agenda for this meeting, focusing essentially upon the range of information required, but she/he will also view this as an early opportunity to gain an initial picture of the school.

Headteachers will also have an agenda. They will want to know the details of the inspection team, and if this has been raised by the staff as a possible source of apprehension then the Head needs to look at the team carefully and be assured that there is an appropriate balance and range of experience. In most cases there will be no problem, but if Heads do feel that there is not the right balance then they may wish to discuss this with the Reporting Inspector. As it is HMCI who actually award the contracts, if schools are very concerned about the composition of the appointed team, it would be appropriate for the governors to write to HMCI indicating any misgivings which they may have.

Headteachers should take this opportunity to put the school into context, to share some information about recent initiatives and developments, and to explore whether the inspection itself can contribute in any way to the school's own identified agenda. For example, if the School Development Plan shows a major area for review in the near future, inspectors may be able to make some helpful observations. Similarly, it could also be a chance to contribute to a school's own evaluation of a recent development. Remember, the inspection team will have a wide range of experience and expertise which could be very useful to the school.

In most cases the Reporting Inspector will spend a day in

the school on this preliminary visit, and a large part of this will be taken up with discussions with the Headteacher. Reporting Inspectors may offer to talk to the staff about the forthcoming inspection at lunch time or after school. It would be worthwhile arranging for the Chair of Governors to join you for some part of the day for some general discussion on inspection arrangements. This would also provide an opportunity for discussion on the use of the parents' response form.

During the course of the day, there will be a need to sort out domestic arrangements for the inspection period. Matters such as car parking arrangements, access to refreshments and arrangements for meeting staff will need to be agreed. If a date has not already been agreed for feedback to the Governing Body following the inspection it would be helpful to arrange this with the Reporting Inspector and the Chair of Governors.

The Reporting Inspector visited on 20 January. I found it interesting how many telephone conversations I had already had with her by then — her calling me. It was almost as if she was trying to get to know me and the school on the phone before she visited. We spent the bulk of the time going through the information pack in detail. In addition she took a staff meeting at which she explained the purpose and process of the inspection and asked the staff if there was anything they were unsure about; she looked around the school and we discussed the practical details of the week. The main ones were the need for the inspectors to have detailed timetables for the week (we did this together at a subsequent staff meeting and I posted copies on to the inspectors), the arrangements for the parents' questionnaire and meeting and which room they could use during the week (mine! which meant I was homeless). The Chair of Governors visited during the afternoon so that she and the Reporting Inspector could meet. The format of the questionnaire and the parents' meeting were discussed with her as well as the general format of the inspection.

Headteacher

Review of Routine Procedures

The impending inspection is an appropriate occasion for a school to remind itself of some of its basic everyday routines. A review of routines will also serve as a useful reminder to all staff. This review should have two main aspects:

- what are the routine procedures?
- is everyone aware of them?

A smooth-running school is a powerful indicator of planning, organization and teamwork.

It would be a useful task to review the following:

- arrangements for supervising pupils before and after school;
- breaktime and lunch time arrangements;
- staff punctuality;
- assembly routines;
- movement around the school;
- marking of registers;
- marking of work;
- requirements specific to safe working such as appropriate dress for PE or art work;
- communication systems;
- behaviour policy.

These areas are common to all staff and should therefore be the subject of clearly understood guidelines.

Timetable of Events

This should be very straightforward. Any events or meetings which bear upon the inspection should be indicated on the action plan. Team and staff meetings should be planned to enable all staff to be kept up-to-date with progress and developments. A final staff meeting, about a week before the inspection, should be an opportunity to reassure staff and to clarify the arrangements for the inspection period.

Date	Event/Meeting	Purpose/Agenda	Person(s) Responsible	Completed (√)
. . . . .	Senior Management Team	General briefing	Head	
. . . . .	Initial meeting with Reporting Inspector	Put school in context Details of inspection team	Head	
. . . . .	Briefing Coordinators	Familiarization with Framework Support and advice	Head Deputy Head	
. . . . .	Staff meeting	Review school systems	Deputy Head	
. . . . .	Curriculum meetings	Review procedures	Curriculum Coordinator(s)	
. . . . .	Governors' meeting	Brief Governors	Head/Deputy	
. . . . .	Year meetings	Review curriculum plans	Year Leaders	

Figure 11: Pre-inspection action plan

Action Plan

The action plan should be a brief and clear summary of the management strategy. The following provides an example of a possible action plan (figure 11). Whatever the format, any plan should be made available to all staff, perhaps by displaying a copy in the staffroom.

Documentation (see Appendix 3)

A wide variety of documentation will be required before and during the inspection period. Some of the inspection team's requirements for documentation, particularly relating to staffing, curriculum and assessment are spread throughout the Handbook. They are summarized below under the appropriate headings. The purpose of the documentation is to inform the inspection team about the context, management and organization of all aspects of the school. On the basis of written information, and briefings from the Reporting Inspector, the team will form an initial view of the school.

The types of documentation required fall into five broad categories. These are:

(i)   basic data
(ii)   general information
(iii)   staffing
(iv)   curriculum
(v)   assessment

Basic Data

Much of this will be supplied through completion of the Headteacher's form which is in the Handbook. Headteachers will need to provide factual information about such matters as school organization, staffing, National Curriculum assessment results, details of finance, accommodation, special needs support, and links with parents.

General Information

This will include a variety of information related to the management and organization of the school. The detail of what is required is listed in the Handbook under 'Guidance on Inspection Organisation'. It includes a range of information on a school's systems, procedures and general policies. This will inform the team on a variety of matters relating to the day-to-day running of the school, and be used as the basis for some discussions with staff, governors and parents.

Staffing

Inspectors will require access to the following:

- job descriptions;
- staff development policy;
- staff handbook;
- staffing policy and structure for teaching and support staff;
- pay policy;
- staff profile and deployment;
- details of staff and working group meetings;
- working party minutes.

Curriculum

Details of the following will be required:

- schemes of work;
- curriculum plans and timetable;
- information on whole curriculum planning;
- curriculum organization and planning including coverage of National Curriculum;
- plans, lesson notes and forecasts;
- balance of time spent on various subject areas.

Assessment

- policy and guidelines;
- teachers' records and reports;
- assessment information and procedures related to the special needs policy.

It is important to note that the Handbook does not give guidance on what some of these terms mean, or what documentation might be expected to include. If you are unclear about what inspectors may mean by whole curriculum planning, or whether schemes of work are what you would refer to as curriculum guidelines, discuss this with the Reporting Inspector at your preliminary meeting, and seek clarification.

Most of the documentation will be required in advance. Working documents such as lesson plans, forecasts and teachers' day-to-day records will need to be available during the inspection itself.

It is unlikely that any school will have appropriate documentation relating to all the areas for which it is required. It is worth bearing in mind that there is little point in writing a policy or a scheme of work merely because the school is to be inspected. As experienced professionals, inspectors will recognize material which is invented or hurriedly devised. Documentation will inform inspection team members of school policy, and will form the basis for evaluating practice. Any written information which has not been shared with staff, or does not guide their work, will soon be revealed as no more than a paper exercise.

However, it is obviously important as part of the preparation for inspection to check on what information is available, to identify gaps, and to make some decisions about appropriate action. There may well be areas of school life where practice is well-established, but not documented, for example in terms of discipline and pupil behaviour. If staff are aware of what is expected, and if their approaches are reasonably consistent, it would be worth recording what amounts to a hitherto unwritten policy.

There will also be areas which the Headteacher recognizes are in need of some major review, and where documentation is outdated or non-existent. This will probably apply to some aspects of the curriculum. The School Development Plan will inform inspectors of those subjects which are planned for review, and they will not be surprised if there is not a scheme of work or written guidance for every curriculum area. It may be helpful to prepare a brief summary statement of the situation in regard to these particular areas to inform the inspection team of current practice and planned developments.

It will be important to be honest with the Reporting Inspector about gaps in any area for which documentation is requested. She/he will be more impressed by a clear account of the reasons for the deficiency, and an indication of your plans to remedy this, than by attempts to cover up the gaps. Talking through the School Development Plan will be useful in this discussion.

As Headteachers read the Framework it will become apparent that there are some significant areas for which documentation might be expected, and which could easily be overlooked. These include provision for all aspects of equal opportunities, which will be commented on within a specific section of the final report.

Certain policies are the responsibility of the Governing Body, and it will be important to clarify these with governors at their briefing meeting. These include an admissions policy, provision for children with special needs, a sex education policy, a budget plan, a complaints procedure and a grievance policy. In the absence of any of these, a Governing Body might act as advised above, in making a brief statement about a particular area after seeking advice from the Headteacher.

The Involvement of Parents

A consistent theme in the educational legislation of the past six years has been the rights of parents which are now laid down in the Parents' Charter. Given this emphasis it is not surprising to find that parents have a significant role to play in the inspection.

Parental views about various aspects of the school will be part of the evidence inspectors will use to make their judgments. This may cause some concern, since clearly the views of parents are often based on limited experience, and few parents can have a picture of the whole school. However, many schools have made great efforts to involve parents not only in their children's learning, but also in the life of the school. It is important therefore, that inspectors receive the views of a range of parents who are involved in different aspects of school life. Their range of experience may cover the following:

- Parent/Teacher Association members (or equivalent);
- parent governors;
- regular parent helpers;
- parents who have accompanied school outings;

- parents involved in reading at home schemes;
- parents who have had home visits.

Some parents find it difficult to become involved in any school activities for a variety of reasons. They will also have an opportunity to give their views through the parents' response form and at the pre-inspection parents' meeting.

The following steps may help to ensure that parents play a positive role in the inspection:

(i)   informing parents
(ii)   explaining their role
(iii) documenting parental involvement
(iv) briefings

Informing Parents

This should be done very early. A simple letter, or perhaps an item in a regular newsletter, could inform them that an inspection will take place and could indicate that they will have an opportunity to contribute to the process.

Explaining Their Role

After consultation with the Reporting Inspector, a further letter should outline clearly how parents will be involved. This should include details about the parents' response form, if it is to be used, and the subsequent parents' meeting. The letter should also indicate those areas about which their views will be sought.

Documenting Parental Involvement

A school's involvement with its parents will be of a varied nature. It would be worth listing this involvement and making it available to inspectors. The documentary information could include:

- pattern and nature of parent consultations;
- activities involving parents;
- schemes which involve parents such as reading or home-work;
- lists of regular helpers and activities in which they are involved.

Essentially, the information should include anything which entails parental involvement or support.

Briefings

Parents or helpers who will be in school during the period of the inspection should be briefed so that they will be prepared to talk about their role to inspectors. It would also be useful if, at an early stage, the Headteacher explained the involvement of parents to the parent governors, and discussed how they might contribute to the inspection process.

The Parents' Meeting

It will be the responsibility of the Reporting Inspector to organize and run the parents' meeting which must be held prior to the inspection period. The 'Guidance: Inspection Organisation' (Part 3) in the Handbook has details of the arrangements for, and the purpose and format of, the meeting. There is also a list of specific issues on which parents' views must be sought. A letter (Appendix B in the Guidance), must be sent to all parents, inviting them to attend the meeting. The main areas on which their views are to be sought include:

- information provided for parents;
- parents' involvement in school;
- pupils' progress and standards achieved;
- values promoted by the school in developing pupils' spiritual, moral and social awareness;
- pupils' behaviour and attendance.

This is by no means an exhaustive list, as parents' views may be expressed on other matters at the meeting.

The letter inviting parents to the meeting will be sent by the appropriate authority for the school, which in most instances will be the Governing Body. Where practicable, parents should have three weeks notice of the meeting. Governors may also, if they so wish, seek the views of all parents using the 'response form' also found in Appendix B of the Guidance. It will be important to agree the arrangements for the meeting with the Reporting Inspector at the preliminary discussion. The Guidance states clearly that there is no legal entitlement for the Headteacher, staff or members of the Governing Body to attend the meeting, unless they are parents of children attending the school.

This type of meeting, openly inviting comments from the parent body on various aspects of school life, will be a totally new experience for many schools. It is important to be clear about the context in which the meeting should take place. The Framework states clearly that 'the meeting will provide valuable background information for the inspection and should be taken into account in the course of the inspection'. Whilst inspectors will note parents' views, they will be in no position to respond to these prior to the inspection. The Reporting Inspector has to make clear to parents at the beginning of the meeting that, whilst their views will be taken into account, they may not necessarily be reflected in the report. She/he must also explain the nature of the inspection to parents, and that explanation should make it clear that a wide range of evidence needs to be sought before arriving at judgments on any aspect of the school. If parents' views are referred to in the report, there must be an indication as to whether the findings of the inspection do in fact support them.

The Reporting Inspector will also make it clear at the outset of the meeting that discussion must be in general terms, and that individuals, whether pupils, staff or governors, are not to be named or to be the subject of particular comments. This is significant in ensuring a professional tone for the meeting, as it should not be an opportunity for a dissatisfied parent to complain about a matter which should be dealt with on an individual basis.

ACTION	DATE	NOTES	DONE (√)
Informing			
Deputy Head (plan staff briefing)			
Staff briefing (special meeting if necessary)			
Chair of Governors (arrange governors meeting(s)			
LEA (if appropriate)			
Parents			
Non-teaching staff			
Planning			
Consult The Handbook			
Allocate roles and responsibilities			
Brief senior teachers			
Brief coordinators			
Brief governors			
Devise action plan			
Plan initial meeting with Reporting Inspector			
Documentation			
Collate			
Identify gaps			
Devise contingency plans			
Involving Parents			
Discussions with parent governors			
Discussion with PTA committee			
Write to parents with further details			
Plan parents' meeting with Reporting Inspector			

Figure 12: Action check list

Almost inevitably, parents attending the meeting will have a range of views on, and understanding of, the running of the school. There is therefore a possibility that some parents will make comments that are based on anecdotal information or are highly subjective. The Reporting Inspector will be only too aware of this, and will place such comments in a balanced context.

The Reporting Inspector will share the findings of the meeting with the Headteacher and Chair of Governors soon after it has taken place.

Action Check List

The various stages of preparing for the inspection include the involvement of different groups and planning a range of strategies for managing the process. These are summarized as an Action Check List (figure 12) which could serve as a useful *aide-mémoire* for Heads and senior teachers.

Chapter 4

The Inspection Itself

Introduction

> The week before the inspection I met a teacher who had recently been part of an LEA inspection. She said that the week before the inspection had been harder than the inspection week itself. I feel the same. It is good to have foreknowledge so that preparations can be made but as the inspection looms larger so the tension grows, a bit like waiting for a race to start.
>
> *Headteacher*

It is perhaps ironic that this chapter which looks closely at the actual period of the inspection is the shortest. In many ways this part of the process will be the least problematic assuming that the preparation has been thorough. However, it is the period when teachers will be under most strain, and so we look at what teachers can expect when inspectors visit classrooms, and also how the Headteacher can help to keep anxieties to a minimum. The chapter is divided into the following sections:

- The Inspection Team in School
- Visits to Classrooms
- Role of the Headteacher

The Inspection Team in School

During the inspection period, the focus of inspectors will be very much on classroom activities during the school day, and this will inevitably create a certain amount of apprehension on the part of teachers.

However thorough the preparatory stages, and however clear staff may be as to what inspection involves, for most teachers this will be a new experience. It will be a very rigorous process, and teachers could become very anxious about the wealth of detail which is required by inspectors in the course of their work.

Essentially, the message for teachers is that inspectors will be concerned with all aspects of school life. One or more of the team is likely to attend assemblies, join children for lunch, be visible during playtimes and around the school to check on routines, observe extra-curricular activities, and may attend staff or curriculum meetings. Children's arrival at school and registration procedures will also be observed. Team members will become involved in discussions with children, parent helpers, ancillary staff, governors and teachers, though possibly very briefly in some cases.

Some aspects of the team's work will be planned in advance, but staff need to be clear that the expectation of inspectors will be that they can go into any classroom at any time.

It may be possible in advance of the inspection to agree outline arrangements for inspectors' discussions with coordinators. Teachers need to be aware of the sorts of areas likely to be raised in discussion so that they can supply relevant information (see Chapter 2).

Visits to Classrooms

Visits to classrooms can be expected at any time during the school day. Teachers should be informed that inspection team members each have a number of areas on which they are gathering information. They will work to a very tight timescale, and because of this may move fairly rapidly from one classroom to another. Preliminary information will inform them of some timetabled activities on which they will focus, but there may well be teaching sessions where they will be in and out, depending on the content.

Essentially, it is important that teachers are clear that during inspection:

- inspectors may visit classrooms at any time;
- they may or may not know in advance of a visit by an inspector;
- short term plans and lesson notes need to be available for inspectors;
- inspectors do not expect to spend time talking to teachers during their classroom visits as they want to see teachers teaching;
- some classes or teachers may receive more visits than others, and this is not necessarily significant;
- inspectors need to produce lesson observation notes for each visit and will spend some time writing in each classroom;
- inspectors may appear uncommunicative, and comments or feedback may be very limited.

The Role of the Headteacher

If the inspection has been well planned by the Reporting Inspector and the Head, during the inspection period itself the Head may feel almost redundant! It is a slightly unnerving feeling to know that your school is under a microscope, and yet you have a limited role in the activities being observed. As with staff, the message for Headteachers is 'carry on as normal'. If you usually have teaching commitments, a regular meeting with the Chair of Governors or a certain time set aside for seeing parents, maintain your routine. Inspectors will not expect you to be continually available to them — indeed if you are, they may begin to wonder about your role in the school!

There will be times when some members of the team will wish to see you briefly to discuss some aspect of the school's work. In order to avoid overloading the Head, team members will usually negotiate meetings through the Reporting Inspector, and a mutually convenient time will be arranged.

During the inspection period the Reporting Inspector will make a point of seeing you at regular intervals. You can normally expect her or him to talk to you at the start of each day and to see you briefly before the team leaves the site each evening.

These short meetings serve three main purposes:

- to check how the inspection is going from the school's point of view;
- to collect any additional information the team might require;
- to begin to informally share some of the inspectors' initial findings.

Inspectors are well aware of the stress on teachers caused by their frequent visits to classrooms. Reporting Inspectors will usually log classroom visits to try to ensure that all classes receive an equitable amount of attention and that no teacher is over-visited. However, if you as Head notice that a particular member of staff is under undue pressure, do inform the Reporting Inspector, so that s/he can take appropriate action. You will also need to make the Reporting Inspector aware of any staff absences, through illness or for in-service, and of supply cover arrangements. Classes covered by supply teachers are likely to be visited, but inspectors are obviously going to make some allowances for this arrangement.

Although you will have supplied very detailed information on the school's timetables and activities during the inspection period, do keep the Reporting Inspector up to date with events. If there are particular activities such as an assembly for parents or a class presentation of a performance, an inspector may wish to attend. The inspection team will want to sample any extra-curricular activities, so an updated list of these will be helpful.

If the school has some part-time teachers, perhaps under Section Eleven or providing support for children with special needs, do ensure that inspectors are aware of the times that they are in school. They will also be interested in any visits planned by members of Learning Support Staff, Advisory Teachers, Educational Psychologists and others who support and advise on pupil learning. Any part-time support given to statemented pupils should be highlighted, as the inspector deployed to look at special educational needs may wish to observe and talk to the person concerned.

An important aspect of the Headteacher's role during

inspection is maintaining staff morale. Teachers will, at the very least, feel uncomfortable about classroom observation and the lengthy notes which inspectors make in the course of their visits. The stress is generally most acute during the first two days. After this teachers begin to get more used to the process, may have had some discussions with inspectors, and will at least recognize them and be accustomed to their presence around the school. Throughout the inspection it is important to give teachers an opportunity to talk through their feelings about the process and for them to use the Headteacher, and Deputy as sounding boards. Try to ensure that the staff get together on a regular basis, probably at lunch time, to share experiences and, if possible, some humour!

The Reporting Inspector may begin to briefly comment on some aspects of the school during the course of discussion and some information could be usefully shared with staff. At a fairly early stage, inspectors will notice such things as pupil behaviour, the general organization of classrooms, and displays around the school and you may receive some positive comments or indication of areas they are identifying as in need of improvement. Where some general positive observations are made, it is useful to pass these on to the staff, so that they are aware that some of their efforts are being recognized.

As the week progresses, inspectors may have some specific requests such as samples of pupil records or profiles being available in every class on a particular morning. Headteachers should ensure that all staff are kept informed of these requirements.

Although in the course of preparing for the inspection, teachers will have been informed of the purpose and process, it may be worthwhile repeating certain messages during this period. Teachers may need to be reassured that inspectors are primarily concerned with gaining an overview of the school, not looking at individual performances. They may also need to be reminded that a very wide range of activities are undertaken by the inspection team in order to arrive at a judgment on an aspect of the school which forms only a paragraph of the final report. For instance coordinators may feel that their role is being closely examined, and so it may be, but this will be only one factor in arriving at judgments on a particular subject. Staff will also need to be clear that inspectors may seem to be making excessive demands for information or documentation, or revisiting classes at frequent intervals. They are not being difficult, but merely trying to check on detail in order to be fair to the school.

Two Headteachers, a Deputy Head and a curriculum co-ordinator have made the following observations on their experiences during inspection.

The Inspection Week

I got to school at 7.50 on the Monday, two of the inspectors had beaten me to it and were making themselves at home in my office. The others arrived shortly afterwards. I had thought that the first morning would be a 'warm up' morning — it wasn't. They were very well prepared and started straightaway.

There seemed to be a very definite psychological pattern to the week. On Monday and Tuesday the school was 'highly charged', the inspectors were very busy both observing in classrooms and interviewing myself and the staff. I told the staff to be open and honest. I had a number of interviews with the inspectors — very much them asking questions and me giving answers. I felt that in one of these I became defensive and asked to repeat the interview the following day which I did. I had some opportunities to discuss issues with the inspectors in a less formal way. In retrospect I got some good ideas from these. I felt that one class reacted badly to the number of visitors. I made a point of spending time in the class every day for the rest of the week.

Wednesday felt like the calm after the storm and was, from my point of view, the best day of the week and the one which showed the school in its best light. The inspectors too seemed much more relaxed.

Thursday was a tired day, both for the staff and I suspect, for the inspectors who worked very hard during the week. I took assembly on Thursday with four inspectors at

---

the back making notes, it made me appreciate what it was like for the teachers.

Headteacher

Reactions and Expectations

When first informed of the inspection, I was naturally apprehensive and concerned, because I had never been involved in a whole school inspection before, although I had had various one day visits from LEA Inspectors. My main concerns were worries about all the correct paperwork being in place, sufficient knowledge about current educational issues, and fulfilling my role(s) properly. I expected the week to be exhausting and stressful, but I also thought it would be good to be assessed as a school and as a teacher, from a professional and personal point of view. I had always found previous encounters with inspectors constructive and helpful, even when critical, and expected the same from a School Inspection.

The three weeks preceding inspection were full of barely controlled panic. When the inspection arrived it was rather like a performance — nerve racking before, but got the adrenalin flowing when it finally happened!

Being Observed

I didn't find it particularly upsetting, as I am used to working with other adults in the room and about the school. All the discussion I had was constructive, and I felt I was talking with people who thoroughly understood the situation and could offer an overview that was helpful. It was odd only to be observed taking maths, (several times) and have no visits for English, which is my responsibility.

Interview

This was quite probing, and all the documentation concerning this area had been read and evaluated. I was questioned quite thoroughly about various practices and statements, but I was able to discuss various points of concern, seek advice, and compare our problems with those of other schools. We discussed English and Special Needs at length, and there were some areas of disagreement, but recognition was given to the fact that we had just moved into a new building and were still experimenting and reorganizing. I felt it was a professional, constructive interview, when I was given plenty of opportunity to explain my views, but also asked some fairly taxing questions that made me think and examine some of my decisions.

Curriculum Coordinator

Although a somewhat false scenario was acted out, in so far as some lessons were presented as 'safe' lessons and there was a slight tendency towards more formal teaching, the week went surprisingly smoothly. The staff, quite naturally relaxed as the week developed. The teachers were very professional and eager for immediate feedback on what had been observed. There was very little grumbling about 'mismatch' of perceptions and during the week the staff felt the confidence to discuss concerns, doubts etc. with the Inspection Team. It was rather more wearing for me as Headteacher for at particular times some documentation or evidence was required and had to be sought immediately.

Headteacher

Monday morning arrived, for all of us, with many reservations. The week before had been spent thoroughly planning each session of the day so as to leave no stone unturned. We were prepared! However, there was a certain edginess about us as we prowled around the corridors waiting for the 9 o'clock whistle. It wasn't long before strangers began to appear and it was obvious the inspection had begun.

At break time the general feeling amongst the staff was, having got over the initial hour, things could only get better. The inspectors obviously had set areas to observe and were straight into classrooms. Prior knowledge of the way they worked helped us in that we knew they would enter a classroom and begin scribing non stop for the period of observation. They were clear as to exactly what they wanted to see as they all had our class timetables highlighting the areas for and times of, observation.

Lunch time was a welcome break. Being a split site school and having two staffrooms it was good for staff morale when it was decided to eat together and share experiences. It was certainly a lively discussion. Throughout the day the inspectors began to bid for the staff's time to interview them with regard to their coordinator and managerial roles. Our break times, lunch hours and after school time was quickly being snapped up.

The final bell at the end of school on Monday came as a great relief. We had definitely felt the pressure.

On Tuesday we felt blitzed from the moment we arrived in school. Soon after 8 o'clock they arrived with clipboards and it was obvious it was their 'accommodation and resources' review morning. Every room, cupboard, drawer and shelf was checked — nothing was left untouched. To be fair, they asked questions rather than taking things on face value and were ready to discuss some basic aspects of their findings. During the morning they were in and out of most classrooms giving a fair coverage to all of us, although some of us felt more blitzed than others. Our spare time was beginning to be eaten into by now as they had begun to conduct their interviews.

By the end of Tuesday both staff and pupils were growing accustomed to these 'additional adults' wandering in and out of classrooms and around the school. The staff had certainly relaxed somewhat and were keen that the inspectors saw all the good aspects of the school. If they had not asked questions on certain issues or observed particular elements of the curriculum, some of us were confident enough to ask them to come and discuss them with us.

It was also certainly very reassuring to have parents come to us at the end of the day and give us support and encouragement. This gave an additional fillip to all concerned.

We had been told that Tuesday was to be their late evening in school. They had requested that the staff should leave out for their perusal the work of three children — this was to be work of a more able child, an average ability child and a less able child. Certainly in my classroom they were scrutinized thoroughly.

Wednesday was certainly interview day. I had an appointment with one of the inspectors at 8.20am. I, and certainly some of my colleagues, felt that the content of these interviews was repeated by different members of the inspection team and was generally unnecessary as it took up some of our valuable time.

I felt by this stage of the week, the staff were coping well. They had accepted the presence of the inspectors and now wanted to show off their planning, even to the extent of hoping that they would receive a visit at that magical moment when something sparkling was happening within the classroom. Inevitably, that moment was missed by the inspecting team and the staffroom discussions often centred around the lessons that were deemed 'howlers' — the camaraderie amongst us was obvious and it was good that the Head was very involved in these vital 'chats' in our one sanctuary, the staffroom.

By the end of Wednesday we began to feel we were nearly there, just one more day to survive.

Thursday was the final countdown. The inspectors went about their observations as normal showing no signs that this was the final day. The staff were still 'charged' but quietly, I know like me, they were battle weary — both physically and mentally. By now most of us had built up a certain amount of rapport with the inspectors and they, in turn, were informally debriefing individual members of staff and/or coordinators as much as they were allowed, which was good as it gave the staff some immediate feedback. We were all desperate to know how we'd done and how the school had faired. It began to give an overall view of the week's inspection.

I also felt that by now some of the impressions and attitudes that certain inspectors had had earlier in the week had perhaps changed through our intervention to show certain aspects of the school. This strategy of intervention had certainly paid off.

There was undoubtedly an enormous sigh of relief when the 3.30pm bell went to signify the end of school. We knew the inspectors had a meeting arranged, so to all intents and purposes the inspection had finished. We had survived. We retired to the staffroom to celebrate this momentous occasion and generally swap stories of the week. It was a good feeling.

The inspection had undoubtedly brought us as a staff closer together, giving strength and support to each other. It had focused our attention on our teaching methods and our learning outcomes and it was obvious we had derived much from this. There is no doubt in my mind that we could not have worked any harder for this week and that we had really pulled out all the stops to show us and the school in a good light.

For their part the inspectors had done their job professionally but with a great deal of sensitivity towards us and the children.

But overall we had SURVIVED and I'm sure that we will all benefit from the inspectors' findings which will give us a way forward for the future which can only be a positive move.

Deputy Head

Chapter 5

Responding to the Inspection

Introduction

This chapter concentrates on the period after the inspection and looks at the range of tasks which need to be done if the inspection is to be beneficial. The timescale is important and so this chapter is divided up into sections which represent the short, medium and long term nature of the school's response. Within each of these periods there is a range of specific activities which have to be undertaken. This chapter is therefore divided up in the following way:

- From Initial Feedback to Feedback to Governors:
  — Initial feedback
  — Reflecting
  — Debriefing teaching staff
  — Debriefing non-teaching staff
  — Head meets with Chair of Governors, and Governors' Meeting
  — Information for parents
- From Feedback to Governors to Publication of Report:
  — Inspectors' feedback to governors
  — Governors' response to the report
  — Establishing governor/staff working parties
- From Publication of Report to Report becoming Public:
  — Informing parents
  — Preparing and distributing a press release
  — Developing detailed action plans

From Initial Feedback to Feedback to Governors

The timing and nature of the feedback will have been negotiated by the Reporting Inspector and the Headteacher at the preliminary visit. The feedback will take various forms. There may be a brief meeting towards the end of the inspection week which simply explores main findings and key issues. This would be followed, perhaps a week later, by a more detailed feedback, focusing on all aspects of the school and the subject areas. On some inspections, the detailed feedback may be given at the end of the inspection week.

Assuming the former pattern, towards the end of the inspection week, the Reporting Inspector, and another member of the inspection team will sit down with the Headteacher and Deputy and report back the early results of the inspection. This may not be a long meeting and inspectors will confine the feedback at this stage to the main findings and the key points for action. In most cases, the main findings will not come as a surprise, as during the week some of this information should have been discussed by the Reporting Inspector with the Headteacher.

It is not, however, the reporting of the main findings which is important but the decisions about how the school is to respond. If the inspection has gone smoothly then the likelihood is that schools will receive the main findings in a positive manner, and indeed they may even become incentives to further development.

Initial Feedback

At the detailed feedback, all parts of the report including whole school aspects and curriculum areas will be discussed with the Headteacher and, in most cases, the Deputy Head. There will be opportunities for the Head to ask questions and to clarify any uncertainties. It is very clear in the Framework that inspectors' judgments must be based on the range of evidence collected in the course of the inspection. There may be some judgment or comments made which Headteachers may wish to dispute, but it must be understood that the inspectors at this stage will not alter their judgments, unless they are based on serious factual errors. Arguing about, or disputing the main findings, is not appropriate; ask for clarification, or maybe ask for some indication of the evidence on which the judgment is made.

It would be worthwhile for the Headteacher to make notes, as inevitably a lot of information will be given, and the pressure of the moment may mean that some points will be lost. Inspectors are not in a position to offer advice, or recommend specific courses of action, but that should not prevent Headteachers asking questions for clarification of particular points, and perhaps trying their own ideas out with the inspectors.

Prior to the feedback with the Headteacher, those inspectors who have looked at specific curriculum areas may have had some discussions with the teachers who have responsibility for those areas. After the feedback sessions it would be sensible to get together everyone who has received feedback and share all the information. It is important at this stage for Headteachers to stress the confidentiality of the inspection findings. Clearly there will be considerable interest amongst the staff, but the findings should not be discussed with parents and other members of the community. Discussions with governors should be conducted initially through the Headteacher. This will help to avoid any potential ambiguity.

The report was given to me (the deputy head was present to take notes) on the Friday after half term. Including a tea and cake break it took $2\frac{1}{2}$ hours. It obviously wasn't possible to take in all the information given, hence the notes, but I had been given feedback during the course of the inspection and therefore there were no surprises (even if I hadn't had the feedback the report would still not have been a surprise, it didn't say anything I don't know). I would have liked the opportunity to debate some of the points they made. Given the length of time it took anyway I can understand their reluctance.

After a break the inspectors then presented the report to

> the Governors. One of them suggested that it would have
> been better if they could have had a copy of the report be-
> forehand.
>
> *Headteacher*

Reflecting

If the inspection has gone well, there may be the temptation to
react quickly, and to begin doing things almost immediately.
However, it is important to bear certain things in mind:

- no matter how well the inspection went, staff will be
  exhausted after being under the microscope, and they
  will need a reasonable period to recover, and to be
  allowed to get back to normal;
- the timing of the inspection could be important in decid-
  ing how quickly the school settles down; a half-term, or
  an end-of-term break will often be needed before teachers
  will feel ready to begin to respond to new initiatives;
- it is important to take time to reflect upon inspection
  findings, and the early post-inspection period should be
  a time for thinking and talking rather than great activity.

Bearing all this in mind, it is important that those people who
were involved in the pre-inspection build-up should be kept
informed about how the process developed and what the outcomes were. There are therefore several key tasks which should
be undertaken very soon after the inspection.

Debriefing Teaching Staff

All staff, teaching and non-teaching, will be anxious to know the
outcomes of the inspection. A full staff meeting should be held
as soon as possible after the inspection week to inform all staff of
the main findings and points for action. This could be undertaken

by the Head, but it may be appropriate to allow some of the curriculum coordinators an opportunity to talk about their particular subject areas. The nature of this meeting will largely depend upon the outcomes of the inspection. In those schools where the main findings are satisfactory or better, staff will be eager and enthusiastic to discuss the results. In those instances where the outcomes are less than satisfactory, then Headteachers clearly need to give some careful thought about how this meeting is handled. Guiding principles should be:

- balance positive and negative comments, and think carefully about the words used;
- say nothing which would enable individuals to be identified;
- decide how much responsibility you as the Headteacher should publicly acknowledge for any shortcomings;
- provide some brief ideas about ways in which things may be improved.

It is important to bear in mind, that no matter what the outcomes, major confrontation, arguments and recriminations at this stage will do nothing to improve the situation. There may have to be some hard decisions made in the future, and some views challenged, but this immediate post-inspection period is not the appropriate time.

In those cases where the majority of the outcomes are satisfactory or better, there are still likely to be some particular areas which are less than satisfactory. If discussion of these would easily identify individuals, then this should not be raised in a whole staff meeting.

In many schools the whole staff meeting at this stage may be sufficient in terms of debriefing staff. However, it may be useful to have a series of meetings either with groups of teachers, perhaps year teams, curriculum teams or indeed individual teachers. In this way, Headteachers can get a clear picture of how the inspection went, and what implications there are for the future. Remember, all this is part of the thinking and talking which should be the major activities during this period.

In some respects it is harder after the inspection than during it because the format of the inspection process means that our response to it was very reactive and because it took so much of our time there wasn't much time left to worry about anything else. After the report it is then up to the school to make a considered response.

There is a lot of information in the report, some good and complimentary, some suggesting areas for improvement. The staff obviously want to know how they got on. Should I tell them everything at once or should I feed it back over a period of time? The complication here was that the report made a clear distinction between the performance of KS1 and KS2. This was the part of it that I didn't like because I felt that it could be divisive. I therefore decided to tell the staff about the general points in the report but I have not yet told them about the specific quality of lessons. I shall do that when I see the final report.

Headteacher

Debriefing Non-teaching Staff

Non-teaching staff will also be eager to learn of the outcomes, since to some extent they will also have been under scrutiny. It would be appropriate to highlight any positive aspects of the school in which they are directly involved. For instance if inspection found pupils well-behaved and sociable at lunch times then that should be passed on. Headteachers can be overwhelmingly positive to non-teaching staff, since in most cases they carry no ultimate responsibilities for the areas looked at in inspection. If some aspect of school activity in which they are involved is found to be unsatisfactory, then these issues need to be discussed at senior management level, and then involve non-teaching staff at the appropriate time.

When giving this early feedback to both teaching and non-teaching staff, it may be appropriate to point out to them that the details are still quite sketchy. This will depend largely on the pattern and timing of the inspectors' feedback. All staff will have some expectation that things will happen as a result of the inspection. This expectancy of change should be encouraged, but at the same time staff should be aware that the school's response will be a measured one, and will be managed at a sensible and realistic pace.

Head Meets with Chair of Governors and Governors' Meeting

As soon as the inspection is completed, the Headteacher should have an early meeting with the Chair of Governors. At this meeting Headteachers will need to share the information from the inspection feedback, and discuss the short term strategies for informing everyone else. The Governing Body will already know of the date of the formal feedback to governors, but it would be useful for the Headteacher and Chair to discuss that occasion in some detail.

Once again the precise nature of this governors' first meeting after the inspection will largely depend upon the nature of the outcomes. In unfavourable circumstances, it is particularly important to maintain close liaison with the Chair, and to begin to discuss a range of responses. The Headteacher and Chair should also begin to discuss how parents are to be informed. Even at this early stage, if there are some serious shortcomings highlighted in the report, the Headteacher and Chair could discuss the possibility of seeking further guidance. This could be provided by an LEA officer/adviser, or an educational consultant. It would be helpful if the person(s) involved had some working knowledge of the school and its particular circumstances, and was familiar with the statutory inspection procedures.

Once these issues have been discussed by the Headteacher and Chair, they should be shared with the full Governing Body at the meeting prior to the inspection feedback.

If the main findings are unsatisfactory then the Governing Body will inevitably be disappointed and concerned. It would be helpful in guiding governors and maintaining their confidence if it is clear that some thought has been given as to how the situation can be improved.

Information for Parents

Parents will have been informed that the inspection is taking place. Some will have attended the parents' meeting, and even more will have filled in and returned the parents' response form. Many parents will have received second-hand reports about 'visitors to the classroom' asking questions and 'writing everything down'. Because of this potential level of involvement it must be a priority immediately after the inspection to inform parents that (a) the inspection is over; and (b) what happens now.

This letter will be quite straightforward if the inspection outcomes are generally favourable and this could be indicated in very broad terms. The letter should not go into any details about the findings of the inspection, which are still confidential. Parents will be interested in what happens next and so it would be helpful to provide the following factual information:

- Date of formal feedback to governors;
- Approximate date of publication of report;
- Date when summary/main findings will be available to parents;
- Plans for making public the governors' formal response to the report.

In the event of the inspection outcomes being predominantly unfavourable, then at this stage it would be more appropriate to keep to purely factual information, as in the details outlined above. This is not to deny the right of parents to know the outcomes, but clearly if there are some serious concerns, then the circumstances in which parents are informed need careful thought and wide discussions with senior staff, governors and perhaps LEA officers/advisers or educational consultants. It is unlikely at this stage that these discussions will have taken place.

The important message — whatever the outcomes — is that parents should be informed. Silence on the part of the school at this point could be misinterpreted, whereas clear concise information will maintain the parents' confidence.

From Feedback to Governors to Publication of Report

Inspectors' Feedback to Governors

This meeting will take place shortly after the end of the inspection. It will occur before the final written report is available, but will represent the collective views and judgments made by the inspection team.

This meeting should only have one agenda item — to receive the feedback from the inspection. The meeting is technically convened by the Chair of Governors, who invites the Reporting Inspector and at least one other member of the inspection team to be present. The meeting should be chaired by the Chair of Governors. As part of the feedback, the Reporting Inspector will explain the procedures of the meeting as follows:

- an inspector colleague will take notes of the meeting. These will include any questions and discussion. The notes will identify, by name, people who contribute to the meeting, and must indicate any commitments to altering factual information made by the Reporting Inspector. These notes will be sent to HMCI after the inspection, as a record of the meeting;
- the feedback will reflect the eventual written report. There will be opportunities for questions and clarification.

The Reporting Inspector will also stress that at this stage the report is still confidential. Initially the governors will be given a brief description of the procedures of the inspection, how the inspection team worked, and the range of evidence they gathered. Inspectors will then spend about sixty minutes going through the findings. The feedback will contain only the information which was communicated to the Head at the end of the inspection period.

At the end of this meeting, the governors should have a very clear picture of the particular strengths and weaknesses of the school, together with some key issues to be addressed to facilitate improvements. These points for action will identify what needs to be done, but will not provide guidance or advice. At the end of the meeting the inspectors will leave, and at this point their work in the school is almost complete. They will finish the report and send copies together with a brief summary to the school and governors. A copy of the report will also be sent to HMCI, together with copies of the Record of Evidence, judgment recording forms, subject evidence forms and lesson observation data. The inspectors should have no further need to visit the school.

Governors' Response to the Report

It is the responsibility of the governors to respond to the main body of the report. When the findings have been presented to the Governing Body, the report will still be confidential and only in draft form. It may be several weeks before it is published. When the report is published, the school will be sent copies together with a summary.

The period after the formal feedback to governors, and the publication of the report could be anything up to seven weeks. During this period the Headteacher, together with the governors, should be very active in planning a course of action for when the report is published. They should be focusing upon formulating the school's detailed response, so that they are in a position to give parents and the media a clear account of how they propose to tackle any key issues, when the report is published. What the school intends to do will form an important part of any communications with parents and the press.

Establishing Governor/Staff Working Parties

By this stage, all those who are involved in the day-to-day running of the school will have a very clear understanding of the contents of the eventual report. Just because the report is not published is not a reason to sit back. It is vital that the school uses this period to prepare for the range of reactions and comment which publication will bring forth. The main task is to begin to put together broad plans for dealing with any major concerns.

This can be approached in several ways, depending on the size and organization of the school. In schools with several members of staff, some of the work can be delegated, in smaller schools, all the staff may need to be involved, together with some governors, and perhaps some outside support.

The key issues are likely to fall within one of the following categories:

Management: this would include issues concerned with resourcing, roles and responsibilities, behaviour and discipline, the school community.

Curriculum: whole school planning, assessment and recording, special needs, particular subject areas, Key Stage or age specific concerns.

Buildings: state of repair, use, and appropriateness.

Once the key issues have been put into broad categories, then tasks can be allocated. For instance, curriculum coordinators should play a major part in formulating plans to deal with curriculum issues, deputies and other senior staff should be involved in management and whole school issues. Governors can also be involved, in particular those who have any specific expertise or responsibilities. If the size of school allows, small working groups could look at the key issues in some detail, and their brief should be very clear — to begin to formulate a course of action which will meet the requirements of the key issues.

There is no need at this stage to go into detailed action planning — that will come later. Each of the working groups should be asked to produce a set of broad proposals which could include the following:

- any in-service required;
- use of staff training days;
- acquisition of new resources;
- advice and support from outside the school;
- in-school support.

Key Issues

'To compensate for the weakness noted in reading and writing, particularly in the upper part of the school, the Head and senior management team should review the responsibility for language development and appoint a person to oversee and monitor the work more directly.'

Working Party Proposals

Members of Group: Headteacher, Deputy Head
Chair of Governors, Chair of Finance Committee
Chair of Staffing Committee

We propose over the next two terms to:

- advertise for an English coordinator
- spend a staff development day looking at reading and writing at Key Stage 2
- request support from outside agencies
- focus further evaluations upon Key Stage 2

Possible resources, (assuming fully devolved budget, including staff development funding):

•	Materials	1,000
•	Outside support	500
•	'B' allowance	2,109
•	Evaluation	300
	Approx. total	3,909

Because there is an issue about a new post the situation will vary enormously from school to school, depending upon the amount of staffing and budget.

Figure 13: A published OFSTED report

The groups could consider possible timescales, and resource implications which may be useful when detailed action plans need to be developed. An example of the kind of outline the working groups could put together is shown in figure 13.

If any of the key issues identified in the inspection report correspond to those already in the School Development Plan, then some of the above may have already been considered and could be reviewed for appropriateness.

Once these proposals are in place, and they have been agreed by the Governing Body in principle, then the school is in a good position to inform parents and the press about the results of the inspection and how they intend to respond.

When everyone has been informed, Headteachers should take time to reflect carefully upon reactions from staff and governors.

They should take opportunities to discuss issues surrounding the inspection report with Headteacher colleagues and outside agencies. These people will often provide an objective view which could help further in formulating the more detailed response.

Since the formal presentation of the inspection report is to the Governing Body, it is actually their responsibility to produce the considered response to the report. We will now look in some detail at how that response can be formulated, taking an actual example from a published OFSTED report.

From Publication of the Report to Report Becoming Public

Informing Parents

The issue of informing parents about the findings of the inspection is going to be a sensitive one.

In the event of the report being satisfactory then the simplest course of action is to make copies of the summary and send one to each parent with a covering letter. The letter should contain the following information:

- the positive aspects of the report;
- the school's response to the report;
- parents' means of access to the full report;
- any opportunities for parents to discuss the report more fully.

Some schools may feel it is appropriate to call a meeting of parents to discuss the report, and details of this meeting should be in the covering letter.

In virtually every report there will be a list of main findings and some key issues or points for action. It is important for any school to indicate to parents that it is taking notice of the report, but at the same time it must also stress the positive aspects so that the confidence of parents is maintained. It would be extremely unwise to emphasize only the positive aspects of the report and not refer to the points for action.

The format of the report is such that the main findings and points for action are highlighted at the beginning, and they represent a very broad overall picture. When writing to parents about the issues raised in the report it would be useful to refer to the main body of the report and make use of the more detailed information.

To illustrate this we can use an example of an actual report written to the OFSTED Framework.

> In English whilst the work is satisfactory at Key Stage 1 (KS1, Years 1 and 2), there are some notable variations at Key Stage 2 (KS2, Years 3 to 6). In particular the oldest pupils' achievement is in reading and writing are unsatisfactory.

This is followed by a further paragraph under Key Issues:

> To compensate for the weaknesses noted in reading and writing, particularly in the upper part of the school, the Head and senior management team should review the responsibilities for language development and appoint a person to oversee and monitor the work more directly.

Any parents, particularly of pupils in the upper part of the school, will be concerned reading the above remarks. It is therefore important to put some of those remarks into the context of the whole report, and also indicate how the school intends to respond to the identified weaknesses.

After a full reading of the report, the picture does become slightly different and there are other remarks within the body of the report which, although not changing the nature of the overall judgments, do create some opportunities to put the recommendations into context. For instance, when commenting upon the unsatisfactory achievement of pupils at Key Stage 2 we find the following:

> This group of children experienced a period of disruption some years previously when, because of the rapid growth of the school, there were difficulties in finding permanent teachers for all the classes.

This provides an opportunity to indicate that the findings of the report, at least to some extent, are the result of a situation which may no longer appertain to the school. There are other comments which would also help to provide a balanced picture. In the section on Quality of Teaching there is the following:

> The work is generally well matched to the pupils' ability, particularly in English and mathematics; it proceeds at a proper pace.

From the section specifically about English:

> English is given a high priority by the teachers and is taught for an appropriate amount of time throughout the school.

and

> Standards in speaking and listening are satisfactory across all classes, as are speaking and handwriting skills.

Using the above information the school can inform parents that the school gives a high priority to the teaching of English, and that some aspects, particularly speaking and listening, are satisfactory throughout the school. The inspection found that all aspects of English were satisfactory at Key Stage 1 and whilst there was a concern that reading and writing was not sufficiently developed in Key Stage 2, this applied to a group of pupils who suffered some disruption earlier in their education through the lack of continuity in teaching staff. The inspection also recommended that the school should appoint a coordinator for English who would be in a position to monitor standards, and develop English teaching throughout the school. The school recognizes these weaknesses and proposes that:

- The next staff development day will look at the development of reading and writing particularly with the oldest pupils.
- The school will advertise for an English coordinator as soon as possible.

By using the full report it should be possible for schools to inform parents of the main findings and recommendations which both recognizes the criticism made within the report, but also maintains their confidence.

Preparing and Distributing a Press Release

For many schools dealing with the press will be the most daunting of the tasks after the inspection. It is quite certain that in the early stages of the OFSTED inspections the press, particularly the local press, will take note of and pass comment on school inspection reports. If past experience, especially the decision to publish HMI reports, is anything to go by, the interest will wane over time. Having said that, it is also the case that an unsatisfactory or poor report will be deemed of more interest than a satisfactory or good one. Unfortunately it will be a case of 'bad news is good news'.

The precise nature of the press reaction is very difficult to predict. It will depend very much on various factors, not least of which will be what other news is available at the time. However, it is likely that unless the report is judging the school to be failing it will not figure in the national press. In most cases schools will have to deal only with their local media.

Many schools have been quite effective in developing relationships with local newspapers, radio and television. The publication of OFSTED reports represents a further reason why all schools should have some kind of contact with local media. If there already exists a relationship, then the publication of the report can be regarded as a further feature. Local newspapers will often welcome a press release, and these can be produced in a similar way to the parents' letter. It should be straightforward and balanced. Most local journalists will accept the press release, and maybe ring up for a comment from the Headteacher or Chair of Governors. If you are feeling particularly pleased with the report then perhaps invite the press in to take a few pictures to accompany the article.

Any press release should be talked through with the Chair of Governors, and circulated to all governors for information. It should be relatively short, about two or three paragraphs, and it should contain a name and contact number.

Unless Headteachers are particularly used to talking to journalists, being asked questions about the report may cause some anxiety. Having a copy of the summary and the press release handy when talking to journalists will help to give some confidence. It is important not to be rushed into giving quick answers; often questions will be leading and presumptuous, and it is important to remain calm. If you are not feeling prepared for the interview, or it comes at an unexpected moment, then it may be better to simply say that you would be delighted to discuss the report, but that it is not a very convenient moment — could you ring back? This will at least give you an opportunity to prepare yourself. The main things to remember are:

- be positive, welcome the report, and be prepared to talk about the good things;
- don't talk about weaknesses, but refer to areas for development;
- keep to generalities; under no circumstances name individual members of staff, but refer to 'the school'.

Refusing to make any comment is not helpful. Anyone reading or listening to an item about the school report rounded off by the reporter saying . . . 'when the Headteacher was asked about the report, she/he refused to comment' will draw their own conclusions.

In the vast majority of cases, informing the press will pass off without incident; in some cases schools will — rightly — wish to give as much publicity as possible to the report. In those few cases where the encounter with the press is unpleasant, then it would be advisable for LEA schools to get in touch with their Local Authority Press Officer, who will be able to give some sound advice. If the situation is particularly difficult then all press enquiries could be directed to the Press Officer.

Finally, it would be advisable for all Headteachers to discuss this area with the Governing Body. It may be the case that some of them could be asked to comment, and they may need some guidance. It would be quite appropriate for the Governing Body to nominate someone who will act as spokesperson so that enquiries to any governor will be automatically passed to the nominee.

Developing Detailed Action Plans

If schools are going to 'make the most of their inspection', then translating the main findings into action plans is important. The point was made very early in the book that schools can adopt a variety of attitudes to inspection, but, to make the most of it, schools should try to see it as a contribution to their own self-evaluation. In other words, a formal school inspection can be one element in a school's audit of its own strengths and weaknesses. If schools do see inspection as part of the audit, then it becomes part of the development process. The main findings and points for action should contribute to the school identifying the next set of priorities in the School Development Plan.

Some of this work will already have begun through the working groups established to put forward the broad outlines of the school's response (see figure 13). In the weeks and months following the inspection report, these broad proposals should be transformed into detailed action plans. The action plans should be working documents, helpful to the working groups and — importantly — brief.

Action plans can take different forms but should indicate the following information:

- the precise nature of the development (long-term aim);
- the person(s) responsible for coordinating the work;
- the timescale;
- targets (short and medium term objectives);
- tasks to be done to achieve targets;
- resource implications;
- success criteria.

There already exists a considerable amount of literature on action planning, and it is not the purpose of this book to repeat what others have written. However there is an increasing amount of evidence concerning development planning and it is worth pausing to consider some of it in a little more detail and to try to learn from experience:

- no amount of planning will guarantee success;
- the action plan should be written in practical terms;
- success criteria
    — are a form of performance indicator;
    — should be simple and recognizable or quantifiable;
    — should help to answer the question 'was the development effective?'
- through using success criteria schools will be able to judge how effective a particular course of action has been;
- use a realistic timescale; the inspection report will highlight a reasonable number of points for action, don't be tempted to try to do everything at once;
- as more funds are devolved to schools, specifically for staff development purposes, then resource management becomes a larger element in development planning.

Action planning can be illustrated by using the example outlined earlier in the chapter. The governors have produced a broad outline of how the teaching of English could be made more effective. This now needs to be translated into an action plan.

The following is one version of an action plan, and closely follows the advice offered to schools by the Department for Education in its two booklets (DFE, 1989 and 1991).

Once the action plan has been developed, it should be shown to all governors and all staff. It may be appropriate to ask the LEA advisory service, or an educational consultant, to consider the plan and comment upon its feasibility.

Action plans should be produced for each of the key issues. As action plans are finalized they should be shown to a meeting of the full Governing Body and then displayed in the staffroom. The example (figure 14) shows a development which takes three terms, even though the original outline plan envisaged only two terms. Schools should be prepared to amend and alter the plan as work proceeds.

PRIORITY: To develop a consistent approach to English teaching KS1–2.	COORDINATOR: Headteacher/English Coordinator	TIMESCALE: 2/3 terms
FIRST TERM Target 1: To appoint a coordinator for English.	**SECOND TERM** Target 2 • To begin to develop whole school policies for English. • To raise awareness of NC English.	**THIRD TERM** Target 3 • To support implementation of guidelines. • To evaluate effectiveness of the development.
TASKS • H/T and Governor produce proposed job specification. • Place advert. • Interview and appoint.	**TASKS** • Coordinator to plan staff development day. • Draft guidelines on Reading and Writing discussed at Staff Meetings. • Involve LEA adviser in INSET day.	**TASKS** • Coordinator given opportunities to work alongside colleagues. • Teachers introduce some new writing strategies — with support from LEA advisers. • Coordinator gives help at planning stages to all staff. • One-day evaluation visit arranged.
SUCCESS CRITERIA • Appointment made.	**SUCCESS CRITERIA** • Successful staff development day (ascertained through evaluation). • Draft guidelines agreed.	**SUCCESS CRITERIA** • Teacher feeling more confident and using a range of strategies (evidence in planning/teaching). • Outcomes of evaluation by LEA adviser.
RESOURCES Interview expenses.	**RESOURCES** • Supply time (2 days) • Advisory time (1 day) • Materials (?)	**RESOURCES** • Supply time (5 days) • LEA adviser time (2 days)

Figure 14: Sample Action Plan

References

DEPARTMENT FOR EDUCATION (1989) *Planning for School Development*, London, HMSO.

DEPARTMENT FOR EDUCATION (1991) *Development Planning — A Practical Guide*, London, HMSO.

Conclusion

Having said earlier that it was very much us giving information rather than discussing practice/issues, I feel that I now have a much clearer idea of the shape of the curriculum and what we need to do. Why? Perhaps it is simply because the inspection forced me to think very hard about the school. I think that the informal discussions helped, I got some good ideas from people who work for other authorities.

The report will have a clear impact on our future School Development Plans.

Lastly, will I be ready for them next time — Yes!

It is important to have clear written policies which on the one hand show how the school is addressing the issues created by the implementation of Government policies and on the other hand which show the school's own style and character (not all ours are written).

It is important to have evidence in the school to show these policies in action.

Because of the comprehensive nature of the inspection it is not possible to duck the difficult issues e.g. we shall have to make our policy on the time allocated to different subjects more definite.

Headteacher

Conclusion

The inspection provided opportunities for me to:

(a) ensure that documentation was as up to date as we could possibly have it;
(b) focus on certain areas which need examination, using eyes which were more objective than ours;
(c) confirm my thinking about 'where we were';
(d) confirm my thinking about 'where we are going';
(e) confirm my thinking about the qualities of my staff, teaching and support, and bring us even closer together;
(f) use the expert advice on offer which gave me pointers towards the future;
(g) feel confident about the development of the school;
(h) see how the school responded under pressure (that also included myself);
(i) have a match of my perceptions generally.

Although we are still at a relatively early stage post-inspection, the report has been invaluable for providing signposts for the future. As a result the following will happen:

(a) the School Development Plan will be reviewed. This will provide many opportunities for each member of staff (or Curriculum Teams) to consider the comments contained in the appropriate curricular sections of the Report and evaluate their own part in the Development Plan;
(b) the Management Team of Senior Staff will consider the management aspect of the Report and again evaluate our current style and practice;
(c) we will balance long term and short term objectives of curriculum, organization and management;
(d) we will prioritize areas — this is vital when we consider the financial implications and also constraints — and also balance these against personal professional development;
(e) we will use the Report's contents about funding

for SEN as a weapon to 'beat' the LEA over re-
duction of funding, although being careful, at the
same time, not to undermine many of the excel-
lent comments of the Report about SEN.
(f) we will use the Report as 'PR' with the community;
(g) we will celebrate what is essentially good practice
and lift the morale and worth of the staff and
develop the good team spirit which has been en-
gendered as a result of the inspection.

Headteacher

As the new national arrangements for inspection come into force,
schools, and indeed inspection teams and OFSTED, will be very
much feeling their way. A clear structure for the new system has
been created through legislation, and the Framework provides
coherence and consistency in inspection arrangements. Undoubtedly there will be some changes in the system in the light
of experience, but these are likely to be in matters of detail rather
than in the overall aims of inspection — to assess the strengths,
weaknesses and educational outcomes of individual schools. There
is no doubt that, in the current climate of public accountability,
regular inspection of all schools will continue for the foreseeable
future.

Given that fact, it cannot be stressed too strongly that there
are benefits to be gained from inspection, apart from meeting
statutory requirements. Schools have the potential to use inspection as part of a longer term process of review and development.
If inspection is to assist with that, it is important that schools are
positive in their approach and proactive in how it is managed.
This ensures that it is used by the school and that inspection is
done with the school rather than to it.

An inspection report published on an individual school should
be part of a review and development process, not an end in itself.
There is no doubt that the reports will be forceful in providing
an objective assessment of schools' strengths and weaknesses and
although the language used within a report may appear bland,
it will convey some powerful messages. Responding to those

messages will be a key task for schools in making best use of inspection.

For the majority of schools, inspection will provide a fair reflection of their current stage of development, although they may not agree with everything in their reports. A report may not tell a school anything new, but it should assist in confirming to a school that it is moving in the right direction and it may help to prioritize planned developments.

As the system is worked and teething troubles are overcome, schools and Headteachers in particular, will learn from each other's experiences and begin to see regular inspection as an important feature in school development.

Assessment, Recording and Reporting (ARR)

The following is a guide to the information which will inform inspection judgments:

- Is there a clear policy for ARR?
- Does the school fulfil statutory reporting requirements? (Circular 14/92)
- Is there clear guidance for teachers about assessing pupil achievement, and are there suggested strategies such as observing pupils, discussion, specific assessment tasks, and a consistent marking policy?
- Is evidence kept which covers a wide range of achievement both academic and non-academic? How are pupil profiles or Records of Achievement used?
- What is recorded? National Curriculum coverage, and/or attainment? How do records relate to SOAs/ATs? How are SAT results used?
- What is the relationship between assessment and planning — does assessment inform future curriculum plans?
- Is there someone responsible for ARR, what is their role, has there been any INSET?
- How are pupils and/or parents involved in assessment?

Special Educational Needs (SEN)

Inspectors will judge that SEN provision is satisfactory or better if they can find evidence of the following:

- Clear whole school policy which has been agreed by staff and governors. The policy should include the following information:
  — how pupils with special needs are identified and defined (does this include able pupils?);
  — what range of support is available (to both pupils and staff);
  — the nature of pupil records;
  — how the policy relates to other aspects of equal opportunities.
- SEN accorded a high status throughout the school. This would be supported by the level of involvement of the senior management team, the status of the SEN co-ordinator, the attitude of all staff and children to pupils with SEN. They will also pay attention to the funding, resourcing and accommodation allocated to SEN.
- A degree of governor involvement.
- A system for monitoring the use of funding for pupils with SEN.
- Appropriate learning opportunities. This would be signi-fied by teachers planning for a range of abilities through a variety of teaching methods, range of outcomes, and differentiated resources.
- Pupils receiving extra support when appropriate. In-spectors will look for a balance of in-class and withdrawal support being offered. They will be particularly concerned

to see that pupils who are withdrawn receive an appropriately balanced curriculum and that work done outside the classroom supports the work done in the mainstream.

- Parents being involved in an appropriate way, with an awareness of their child's specific difficulties and the nature of support they are receiving. It may also be the case that they themselves form part of the support through activities undertaken at home.

Documentation

Some schools may feel daunted by the amount of documentation requested by the Reporting Inspector. Much of the documentation will be straightforward factual information, but most schools will have some gaps.

Inspectors are looking for simple straightforward information about how the school operates. The Headteacher's Form will provide much of this, but they will still require other bits of information which will help them form their inspection agenda.

For many Headteachers the biggest task will be collating information since various items will be filed quite separately — for example, information concerning governors will be separate from curriculum planning which, in turn, will be separate from staff information. One thing is certain, those schools which have an up-to-date and efficient filing system will have a considerable advantage in the run-up to inspection.

The following provides some guidance about specific documentation relating to staffing and curriculum.

Documentation Relating to Staff

Job descriptions: These should be the result of negotiation between the Headteacher and postholder. Job descriptions should be brief, clear and quite specific. They should show the title of the job, the purpose of this job, key tasks to be undertaken and the relationship between the postholder and other members of staff.

Staff development policy:	This should give details of: — staff development funding — INSET courses attended by members of staff — staff training days (in recent past and near future) — staff development interviews — teacher appraisal schemes — any induction procedures
Staff handbook:	This could contain any information useful for staff about procedures, policies, systems and guidelines. In some respects summary information relating to staffing and curriculum could form the basis of a staff handbook.
Staffing policy:	This should include teaching and non-teaching staff. It should detail a staff list showing teaching responsibilities, and management responsibilities.
Staff profile and deployment:	This will be entered on a pro-forma contained with the Headteacher's Form.

Documentation Relating to Curriculum

There are no standard definitions of terms such as schemes of work, or curriculum guidelines. Inspectors will be interested in the following information, which should appear in a variety of documentation:

- a broad outline of what pupils are entitled to in National Curriculum subject terms in each age group;
- an indication of which subjects will be covered discretely, or as part of a topic;
- policies concerned with teaching and learning;
- any information which indicates the percentage of time spent on different subject areas;
- curriculum provision — especially relating to the development of numeracy and literacy;
- examples of teacher medium-term planning.

Inspectors will also want teachers' short-term plans to be available and will be looking for evidence of:

- clear relationship between school planning and teacher planning;
- clear learning objectives (related to National Curriculum);
- an approach to differentiation;
- arrangements for assessment;
- a range and balance of teaching and learning strategies.

Making the Most of
your Inspection:
Primary

Other Title in the Series

Making the Most of your Inspection: Secondary
David Clegg and Shirley Billington